Teaching
Children

CHRISTLIKE
VIRTUES
in the Home

Teaching Children CHRISTLIKE VIRTUES in the Home

By
Lily Stainback

Horizon Publishers
Springville, Utah

This is not an official publication of The Church of Jesus Christ of Latter-day Saints. The opinions and views expressed herein belong solely to the author and do not necessarily represent the opinions or views of Cedar Fort, Inc. Permission for the use of sources, graphics, and photos is also solely the responsibility of the author.

ISBN 13: 978-0-88290-844-1

Published by Horizon Publishers, an imprint of Cedar Fort, Inc., 2373 W. 700 S., Springville, UT 84663
Distributed by Cedar Fort, Inc., www.cedarfort.com

LIBRARY OF CONGRESS CATALOGING-IN-PUBLICATION DATA

Stainback, Lily.
Teaching Christlike virtues in the home / Lily Stainback.
    cm.
ISBN 978-0-88290-844-1
1. Virtues. 2. Christian education—Home training. 3. Church of Jesus Christ of Latter-day Saints—Doctrines. 4. Mormon Church—Doctrines. I. Title.

BV4630.S83 2008
241'.4—dc22

2008010673

Cover design by Nicole Williams
Cover design © 2008 by Lyle Mortimer
Edited and typeset by Jessica Best

Printed in the United States of America

10 9 8 7 6 5 4 3 2 1

Printed on acid-free paper

Dedication

I would like to dedicate this book to my best friend and eternal love, Jay. Also to Nick, my hero; Rachael, my inspiration; Wil, our source of never-ending surprise; and Faith, our family's joy.

Table of Contents

Preface

Each chapter in this book covers a Christlike virtue. For each one there is a story from the scriptures. We can learn much from reading about these people who loved the Lord. These stories are summarized in a factual way because often families will have different outlooks on the same story; we don't all receive identical impressions when studying the scriptures. One of my favorite things about the gospel is how personal it is. Heavenly Father speaks to us individually through the scriptures. Encourage your family to discuss the different insights they may have as you study together.

I also encourage you to look at maps as you study the scriptures to increase understanding. Timelines are also useful for putting people, places, and events into perspective. A simple timeline made from poster board cut in half can be hung in your home and added to as you study the scriptures together.

Your family may want to have a Virtue Scrapbook to go along with each activity. Take photographs of crafts you make and activities and store journal entries. Certain lessons encourage you to work on the scrapbook, but you could make it a regular part of each family home evening by devoting time at the end of each lesson This scrapbook will become a family treasure that you can return to time and time again. By studying the virtues of the Savior, we can grow closer to Him and strive to be more like Him. Our Savior lived a life of perfection. He even instructs us, "Be ye therefore perfect, even as your Father which is in heaven is perfect" (Matthew 5:48). The best way, then, to achieve that goal is to pattern our lives after His. Virtue is defined as moral excellence.

This study of the virtues of our Savior has been a beautiful experience for my family, and I hope it will be for yours.

1. Kindness

Definition: Good will; benevolence; disposition that delights in contributing to the happiness of others.

Song: "Kindness Begins with Me" (*Children's Songbook*, 145)

Scriptures: Ephesians 4:32; 3 Nephi 22:8; D&C 4:6

The Parable of the Good Samaritan
Luke 10:25–37

Jesus spent much of His mortal ministry traveling to different areas to teach the gospel. He taught many lessons in the form of parables. The parable of the good Samaritan is a beautiful example of a lesson in kindness.

Jesus was in Galilee teaching and healing. A lawyer stood in the midst of the people and asked how he could obtain eternal life. Jesus responded by inquiring of the man what the Mosaic law said on the subject. The lawyer answered, "Thou shalt love the Lord thy God with all thy heart, and with all thy soul, and with all thy strength, and with all thy mind; and thy neighbor as thyself" (Luke 10:27). Jesus told the man that he was correct, but the lawyer continued, asking, "Who is my neighbor?" (v. 29). It was in answer to this question that the parable of the good Samaritan was taught.

Jesus told of a man that was traveling from Jerusalem to Jericho. He was attacked by thieves who stripped him, beat him, and left him for dead on the road. A priest came along and, on seeing the man lying there, crossed to the other side of the road and kept going. The next man to pass that way was a Levite. The Levites were men who assisted the priests and, in fact, were sometimes called priests themselves. This Levite man happened upon the injured traveler, looked at him, and also crossed to the other side and went on his way.

Finally there came a Samaritan. The Samaritans were a faction who had had bitter struggles with the Jews in times past. There was great contention between these groups of people. This Samaritan, who was traveling on the road where the injured man lay, stopped. He looked at the man and had compassion for him. The Samaritan bandaged the man's wounds, put him on his animal, and took him to a nearby inn. He cared for the man and the next day gave the innkeeper money to continue the man's care. He even went so far as to tell the innkeeper that if the man's expenses came to more than the Samaritan had provided, he would pay the remaining costs on his next trip.

At the conclusion of the parable, Jesus asked the lawyer, "Which now of these three, thinkest thou, was neighbour unto him that fell among the thieves?" (Luke 10:36). The lawyer answered that, of course, the man who had assisted the injured was the good neighbor. Jesus said, "Go, and do thou likewise" (v. 37). This was an especially strong lesson—the Samaritans were considered by many Jews in the area to be unclean.

The Savior taught then, and now, that we are all children of our Heavenly Father. We are to care for one another regardless of any circumstances.

Journal Prompt: Write in your journal what kindness means to you. Can you remember a specific time someone showed you kindness? Look for little acts of kindness you can perform for those you come in contact with throughout the week. Record your experiences in your journal.

Activity: As a family, begin a Virtue Scrapbook. You might include pictures or drawings of family and friends who illustrate the virtue of kindness. Add pages to this scrapbook about different virtues as you progress through this book.

2. Cleanliness

Definition: Freedom from dirt or filth; purity.

Song: "The Lord Gave Me a Temple" (*Children's Songbook,* 153)

Scriptures: 2 Nephi 25:16; Alma 5:19; Moroni 6:4

The Healing of Naaman
2 Kings 5:1–14

The story of Naaman is one of cleanliness for many reasons. Naaman was a nobleman in the court of the King of Syria. The scriptures tell us that he was "a great man with his master, and honourable . . . he was also a mighty man in valour, but he was a leper" (2 Kings 5:1). Leprosy is a dreadful disease of the peripheral nerves and skin that was thought to be highly contagious. The Bible Dictionary tells us that the disease was regarded as a living death.

Many people in this area had been taken captive through the various wars. Among these prisoners was a young Hebrew girl who became a servant to Naaman's wife. This girl told Naaman's wife of the prophet Elisha who could heal Naaman's leprosy. The Syrian king encouraged Naaman to travel to the land of Elisha and even offered to send with him a letter to the king of Israel requesting that Naaman be healed. When Naaman arrived, the king read the letter. Realizing that he did not have the power to heal Naaman, the king became very disturbed.

Elisha heard about the king's dilemma. He came before the king and said of Naaman, "Let him come now to me, and he shall know that there is a prophet in Israel" (2 Kings 5:8). Naaman came to Elisha's house. Elisha sent out a messenger to tell Naaman to go to the River Jordan and wash himself seven times. This angered Naaman, who expected Elisha to come out and dramatically heal him. Naaman was insulted that he had been instructed to bathe in the River Jordan. He said, "Are not Abana and Pharpar, rivers of Damascus, better than all the waters of Israel?" (v. 12). Naaman stormed away, but his servants begged him to stop. They told him that if Elisha had asked him to do some great and complicated thing in order to be healed he would surely have done it. Why, then, they questioned, would he not do this simple thing? Naaman consented. "Then went he down, and dipped himself seven times in the Jordan . . . and his flesh came again like unto the flesh of a little child, and he was clean" (v. 14).

Naaman was cleansed outwardly of his leprosy. More importantly, though, Naaman was cleansed of unbelief and pride. We should keep ourselves clean on the outside by caring for our bodies and following the Word of Wisdom. We must keep ourselves clean on the inside by following the commandments and striving each day to become more like our Savior.

Journal Prompt: Write about what you can do to keep your body and your spirit clean.

Activity: Sometimes Heavenly Father asks us to do simple things. For example, we have been instructed by prophets to plant a garden. Take some time as a family to plant and care for vegetables or fruits to help feed your family and others. Container gardening is a good option if you have limited space.

3. Commitment

Definition: To give in trust; to put into the hands or power of another; to pledge; to be bound to a certain action.

Song: "Dare to Do Right" (*Children's Songbook,* 158)

Scriptures: Deuteronomy 6:5; 1 Nephi 3:7; D&C 4:2

The Fiery Furnace
Daniel 3

King Nebuchadnezzar of Babylon had come to Jerusalem and conquered it. In the conquest, many people were taken prisoner. Among these were three young men named Shadrach, Meshach, and Abed-nego. Nebuchadnezzar had been so impressed with these young men that he had put them in charge of a portion of Babylon. The Babylonian people were very different from the Jewish people. The Jews believed in and worshipped Heavenly Father. The Babylonians built idols of gold and other precious metals to worship. Nebuchadnezzar had a golden statue erected. He called his people together and had it announced that at a signal, which was many musical instruments being played at once, all the people were to fall down and worship this idol. Nebuchadnezzar stated that if anyone refused to obey his decree, that person would be immediately thrust into a great furnace of fire. The music sounded and all the people fell down and worshipped the idol.

A group of people from a southern part of Babylon known as the Chaldeans came to Nebuchadnezzar and told him that Shadrach,

Meshach, and Abed-nego, as Jews, were not following the command to worship the golden image. Nebuchadnezzar was enraged. He had the three men brought to him. Nebuchadnezzar asked them, "Is it true, O Shadrach, Meshach, and Abed-nego, do not ye serve my gods, nor worship the golden image which I have set up?" (Daniel 3:14). Nebuchadnezzar then ordered the three men that upon the signal they must worship this idol or be thrown into the furnace. He added further, "And who is that God that shall deliver you out of my hands?" (v. 15).

At this point, Shadrach, Meshach, and Abed-nego had an opportunity to preserve their lives. They were, however, more committed to God than to life itself. Their answer was, "If it be so, our God whom we serve is able to deliver us from the burning fiery furnace, and he will deliver us out of thine hand, O king. But if not, be it known unto thee, O king, that we will not serve thy gods, nor worship the golden image which thou hast set up" (vv. 17–18).

Nebuchadnezzar was so angry that he ordered his men to heat the furnace to seven times its original temperature. He had the strongest men in his army bind Shadrach, Meshach, and Abed-nego and put them into the furnace. The heat was so intense that the soldiers were killed as they thrust in the bound men. But then Nebuchadnezzar jumped up in astonishment and asked, "Did not we cast three men bound into the midst of the fire?" (Daniel 3:24). His advisors told him that they certainly had. Nebuchadnezzar cried, "Lo, I see four men loose, walking in the midst of the fire, and they have no hurt; and the form of the fourth is like unto the Son of God" (v. 25). The king called for the men to come out. Shadrach, Meshach, and Abed-nego emerged from the furnace without injury. In fact, they didn't even smell like smoke!

These young men never strayed from their commitment to God, even in the face of death. Not many of us are called to make that particular choice, but we do face challenges daily that test our commitment to the gospel. By standing up for what we believe, we prove ourselves to Heavenly Father.

Journal Prompt: Copy the song "Dare to Do Right" in your journal and write about a "work that no other can do" and how you can "stand like a hero."

Activity: Make a suncatcher to help you remember this story about courage. You will need:

black construction paper
wax paper
red, yellow, and orange crayons
an iron, a butter knife or plastic knife
a small towel
hole puncher
string or yarn
silhouette pattern (see appendix)

Using the knife, gently scrape the crayons until you have a small pile of shavings. Trace the silhouette pattern onto the construction paper and cut it out. Place the silhouette on a piece of wax paper. Sprinkle crayon shavings around the figures. Top with a second piece of wax paper. Cover with a towel (to protect your iron) and iron over the surface to melt the crayon wax. Trim around the silhouette as desired. Punch a hole in the top, string yarn through, and hang in a sunny window.

4. Valor

Definition: Courage; in regard to danger a strength of mind; personal bravery; courage.

Song: "Let Us All Press On" (*Hymns*, 243)

Scriptures: 1 Nephi 22:15–17; D&C 6:33–37

Captain Moroni
Alma 43–44, 46

Many years before Jesus was born, two major groups of people on the American continent, the Nephites and the Lamanites, fought wars with one another. The Nephites tried to defend themselves against the wicked Lamanites who sought to destroy them.

At this time a young man only twenty-five years old was chosen to lead the Nephite armies. His name was Moroni. Captain Moroni was a gifted soldier. He led his troops into battle with more advanced weapons and protective gear than the Lamanites had ever seen. The Lamanite army far outnumbered Moroni's, but the Nephites were so much more prepared than the Lamanites that the startled Lamanite army fled into the wilderness. The young captain proved to be wise and sent out spies to follow the Lamanites. In addition to this military move, Moroni made the most important decision: he wanted to consult with the prophet, so he sent word to Alma.

Moroni trusted in Heavenly Father and His holy prophets. He desired to know if the Lord would have him defend his people by pursuing the

Lamanites. Alma prayed and received the answer that the Lamanites were marching through the wilderness in order to attack a weaker Nephite land. Moroni left some of his soldiers where they were to guard the land and took other troops to protect the Nephite land of Manti, which was now in danger. Moroni warned the Nephites in Manti of the approaching Lamanite army and strategically placed his soldiers in the surrounding area.

As the Nephite armies established camp, Moroni sent out spies to watch for the Lamanites' arrival. The spies determined the Lamanites' route, and Moroni placed his men to surround the Lamanite army as they came upon Manti. The Lamanites approached and, seeing the Nephite army, tried to flee. But they discovered that they were surrounded. Fighting broke out. Because they were not as well-armored as the Nephites were, many Lamanites were killed.

The Lamanites fought with fierceness; "nevertheless, the Nephites were inspired by a better cause, for they were not fighting for monarchy nor power but they were fighting for their homes and their liberties, their wives and their children, and their all, yea for their rites of worship and their church. And they were doing that which they felt was the duty which they owed to their God" (Alma 43:45–46).

As the battle continued, the Lamanites began to beat back the Nephites. Their strength and courage began to fail and they even considered giving up and running, but,

> Moroni, perceiving their intent, sent forth and inspired their hearts with these thoughts—yea, the thoughts of their lands, their liberty, yea, their freedom from bondage.
>
> And it came to pass that they turned upon the Lamanites, and they cried with one voice unto the Lord their God, for their liberty and their freedom from bondage.
>
> And they began to stand against the Lamanites with power; and in that selfsame hour that they cried unto the Lord for their freedom, the Lamanites began to flee before them. (Alma 43:48–50)

The Nephite army surrounded the Lamanites, and Moroni ordered that the bloodshed end. He called the Lamanite leader to him and offered their terms of surrender.

Moroni said if the Lamanites would surrender their weapons to him with a promise not to raise them again against the Nephites, he would allow them to leave unharmed. If, however, they did not agree to these conditions, the Nephite army would slay them all. The Lamanite leader, Zerahemnah, refused. He tried to attack Moroni. One of the Nephite soldiers defended Moroni and in so doing, injured Zerahemnah. Instead of surrendering, Zerahemnah stirred up his people to anger. "And now Moroni was angry, because of the stubbornness of the Lamanites" (Alma 44:17). He sent his soldiers to destroy the Lamanites just as he had warned them he would do.

Finally, Zerahemnah agreed to the surrender when he saw that his people were going to be completely destroyed. The Lamanites gave up their weapons and vowed not to battle the Nephites again. Moroni allowed the remainder of the people to go unharmed. The Nephite people rejoiced in the Lord for their rescue from the hands of the Lamanites.

The next year, a man named Amalickiah who wanted to be the king began to lead some of the Nephites in rebellion against the teachings of the Lord. Amalickiah succeeded. "Thus we see how quick the children of men do forget the Lord their God, yea, how quick to do iniquity, and to be led away by the evil one. Yea, and we also see the great wickedness one very wicked man can cause to take place among the children of men" (Alma 46:8–9).

When Moroni heard of these happenings, he was devastated. He was so upset that he tore his clothing, as was the custom of the day to show great distress. Moroni took the torn portion of his coat and wrote upon it: "In memory of our God, our religion, and freedom, and our peace, our wives, and our children" (Alma 46:12). He took this "title of liberty" and attached it to the end of a pole to make a flag. He put on his armor and knelt down on the ground to pray. Moroni prayed that the Lord would preserve the freedom of his brethren and his land as long as there were at least a few who still believed in Christ. He then rode out among his people waving the banner he had made so that the people could read the writing on it. He cried out for all who would be willing to support this cause of freedom to join him. The people came running out after him, tearing their clothing as a symbol of their commitment. They dropped their torn garments at Moroni's feet and promised to follow Heavenly Father or be destroyed.

Amalackiah feared the growing number of Nephites who joined Moroni. He took his few followers and fled. Moroni and the Nephites pursued Amalackiah and required them to enter into the same covenant they had made. Moroni "caused the title of liberty to be hoisted upon every tower which was in all the land, which was possessed by the Nephites; and thus Moroni planted the standard of liberty among the Nephites. And they began to have peace in the land" (Alma 46:36–37).

Moroni never wavered from the gospel. He showed bravery and courage in the face of danger. He showed commitment to the Lord. In times of adversity, Moroni's first responses were to follow the prophet, pray, and then act. Moroni shows us a moving example of the kind of valor our Savior would have us exhibit.

Journal Prompt: Write in your journal your thoughts about freedom. What does freedom mean? What are some freedoms you enjoy? How do you feel about Moroni's commitment to freedom?

Activity: Create your own title of liberty. Use cloth, paper, or any other material you can write on. Write out Moroni's title of liberty and attach your banner to a stick or small dowel. Display your title of liberty in your home and discuss what freedom means to you.

5. Forgiveness

Definition: The act of forgiving; pardoning an offender.

Song: "Did You Think to Pray?" (*Hymns,* 140)

Scriptures: Exodus 34:7; Psalm 32:5; Isaiah 1:18; Matthew 18:21–22

Parable of the Prodigal Son
Luke 15:10–32

One of the many parables Jesus taught was the prodigal son. The word *prodigal* means someone who spends money extravagantly. Jesus prefaced this parable by telling the multitude that had gathered, "I say unto you, there is joy in the presence of the angels of God over one sinner that repenteth" (Luke 15:10). He then proceeded to instruct the people (and us) on how to live the principle of forgiveness.

A father had two sons. The younger son asked his father to give him his part of his father's estate. When the father granted his son's request, the young man ran off and squandered his portion of the estate in what the scriptures call "riotous living" (Luke 15:13).

The son had no money left and, even worse, there was a famine in the land. He found work feeding pigs. The wayward man was so hungry that he would have gladly eaten the seedpods of the carob trees from which the pigs ate. This was humbling for the younger son, and we are told that he "came to himself" (Luke 15:17), which is to say that he realized his foolishness.

As he pondered his situation, he realized he could go home. He felt sure he had done such unforgivable things that he would never be welcomed as his father's son, but he thought that perhaps he could be a servant in his old home. He planned to apologize to his father by saying, "Father, I have sinned against heaven, and before thee, And am no more worthy to be called thy son: make me as one of thy hired servants" (Luke 15:18–19).

Mustering his courage, the son headed home. The father saw his son approaching, ran to him, and kissed him. The son told his father what he had carefully rehearsed in his mind. In answer, the father called for his servant and ordered him to bring out the best robe, a ring, and shoes for his son. He further requested that their best calf be killed for a feast in honor of his son. The father said, "For this my son was dead, and is alive again; he was lost, and is found" (Luke 15:24).

There was a great party going on when the elder son arrived. He called upon a servant to find out what was happening. The servant explained that the younger brother had returned and their father had ordered the festivities. The older son was angry about the reception his younger brother had received; so angry, in fact, that he refused to go in to the party. The father came out to inquire after him. The elder son questioned his father's judgment, saying, "Lo, these many years do I serve thee, neither transgressed I at any time thy commandment: and yet thou never gavest me a kid, that I might make merry with my friends: But as soon as this thy son was come, which hath devoured thy living with harlots, thou hast killed for him the fatted calf" (Luke 15:29–30). The older son had such anger in his heart that there was no room for forgiveness.

His father responded with love and tenderness, saying, "Son, thou art ever with me, and all that I have is thine. It was meet that we should make merry, and be glad: for this thy brother was dead, and is alive again; and was lost, and is found" (Luke 15:31–32).

The Savior used this parable to illustrate the elements of forgiveness through each of the three men. The younger son displays humility in the face of guilt. The father shows us how to forgive without judging. The elder brother demonstrates the dangers of an unforgiving heart. We can learn much from each of these men, but most especially from the teacher—our Elder Brother.

Journal Prompt: Have you ever found it difficult to forgive someone? What helped you overcome that difficulty? How do you feel when you forgive?

Activity: As a family, read "The Healing Power of Forgiveness" by President Faust (James E. Faust, "The Healing Power of Forgiveness," *Ensign*, May 2007, 67–69). Discuss the moving story he recounted of the Amish community's example of forgiveness. Write down a personal and a family goal concerning forgiveness.

6. Honesty

Definition: Moral disposition to follow correct principles; fairness; truth.

Song: "Do What Is Right" (*Hymns,* 237)

Scriptures: Deuteronomy 6:17–18; Articles of Faith 1:13

The Great Spirit
Alma 17–18

The sons of Mosiah left their home to serve missions for the Lord. Their mission calls were similar to those of today's young men and women; they were to go into a different land and share the gospel with all those who would listen.

The four brothers traveled together for some time. As they entered the land of the Lamanites, they split up. Each of the four brothers went his own way, anxious to preach the word of the Lord to the wicked Lamanites, whom the scriptures tell us were "a wild and . . . a ferocious people" (Alma 17:14). Ammon and his brothers were, nevertheless, eager to reach these people with the message of the Savior.

Upon reaching the Lamanite land called Ishmael, one of Mosiah's sons, Ammon, was immediately captured, bound, and taken before the king. King Lamoni questioned Ammon about why he came to Ishmael. He asked if Ammon wished to live with the Lamanite people. When Ammon said he did want to stay, King Lamoni was so pleased that he offered Ammon one of his daughters to wed. Ammon humbly replied that he would be King Lamoni's servant instead.

Ammon's job was to keep watch over the king's flocks of sheep. This was an especially difficult assignment because there had been Lamanites assaulting the king's servants and scattering the flocks.

Ammon and the other servants took the sheep down to the river for water and, as usual, the Lamanite enemies attacked the little group of men, running off the sheep. King Lamoni's servants were terribly afraid that they would be put to death for losing the flocks. Ammon calmly reassured the men, telling them to "be of good cheer" (Alma 17:31). He encouraged the servants to search for the lost sheep and bring them back into the fold to avoid incurring the king's wrath. As the sheep were rounded up, the troublesome band of Lamanites reappeared. Ammon told the men to encircle the sheep while he dealt with the troublemakers. The band of men tried to battle Ammon, but the Lord helped Ammon prevail. Ammon drove away the wicked Lamanites and, with the other servants, delivered the king's flocks safely home.

King Lamoni called his servants to come to him. In amazement, the servants related the story. King Lamoni was astonished by Ammon's apparent strength in fending off the Lamanites. He said, "Surely, this is more than a man. Behold, is not this the Great Spirit who doth send such great punishments upon this people, because of their murders?" (Alma 18:2). His servants replied that they didn't know if Ammon was the Great Spirit of whom their people had been taught, but he seemed to be invincible. They added that Ammon had proven himself to be a great friend to the king. King Lamoni said, "Now I know that it is the Great Spirit; and he has come down at this time to preserve your lives, that I might not slay you as I did your brethren. Now this is the Great Spirit of whom our fathers have spoken" (v. 4).

King Lamoni asked his servants where Ammon could be found. They told him that Ammon was feeding the king's horses. King Lamoni was more amazed than ever, for he could scarcely believe that the supposed Great Spirit would be the king's most humble and obedient servant. He had Ammon summoned to him but was so afraid that he didn't even speak when Ammon arrived and asked what was desired of him. Ammon waited over an hour for a response until, being filled with the Spirit of the Lord, he knew the thoughts of the king. He knew how amazed the king was with his actions and asked, "I say unto you, what is it, that thy marvelings are so great? Behold, I am a man, and am thy servant; therefore, whatsoever thou desirest which is right, that will I do" (Alma 18:17). The fact that Ammon could read the king's thoughts did nothing to assuage the esteem in which the king held him. The king was more convinced now than ever that this man was, in fact, the Great Spirit. He overcame his fear long enough to inquire if Ammon was. Ammon answered simply that he was not the Great Spirit.

Lamoni could not understand Ammon's ability to withstand the forces of the evil Lamanites, humbly submit to the orders of a king, and read the thoughts of his heart. He offered Ammon anything he desired in exchange for the knowledge of his talents.

"Now Ammon being wise, yet harmless, he said unto Lamoni: Wilt thou hearken unto my words, if I tell thee by what power I do these things? And this is the thing that I desire of thee" (Alma 18:22). Ammon's honesty in the face of a possible temptation of fame and fortune provided him with a blessing that far outweighed any earthly reward. He performed great missionary service and worked miracles in the name of the Lord among the Lamanites. This was the righteous desire of his heart, and the Lord blessed him for his efforts.

Honesty is one of those most important virtues that help us to become more like our Savior. There is no amount of wealth or fame in all the world that is worth so much as your good, honest name.

Journal Prompt: Honesty is an important quality. Without it, you can lose the trust of those around you. Write about how important honesty is in your life. Think of a story that portrays honesty (for example, "Honest Abe" Lincoln) and write about it in your journal.

Activity: Find old filmstrips (yard sales and consignment shops are great places for these) and soak them in bleach for a few minutes. Once the pictures begin to come loose, rinse the strips in warm water until they are clear. Wipe dry, then make your own scripture story filmstrip with permanent markers. You can use this activity with any story.

7. Patience

Definition: Suffering afflictions, pain, or provocation with a calm temper; enduring without murmuring.

Song: "God Speed the Right" (*Hymns,* 106)

Scriptures: Psalm 37:7; Proverbs 16:32; 1 Thessalonians 5:14; Alma 38:12

Nephi and His Brothers
1 Nephi 3, 7

Six hundred years before the birth of Jesus Christ, there was a prophet in Jerusalem named Lehi. Lehi warned the people that their city would be destroyed if they didn't repent of their wickedness. When the people refused to listen, the Lord told Lehi to take his family and flee into the wilderness.

The family, which consisted of Lehi; Sariah, his wife; and their children Laman, Lemuel, Nephi, and Sam, departed from Jerusalem with only the most necessary of their belongings. Once they had made camp, the Lord told Lehi to send his sons back to Jerusalem to get the record of their ancestors that had been engraven upon plates of brass. These plates were in the hands of a wicked man named Laban.

Laman, Lemuel, Nephi, and Sam obeyed their father and left for Jerusalem. Upon arriving, they approached Laban and requested the plates. Laban refused. He ordered them to leave and then sent soldiers after them. Laman and Lemuel were angry with their father for sending them on this mission and with Nephi and Sam for supporting their father. Laman and Lemuel were so angry they beat their brothers with a stick. An angel appeared unto the elder brothers and commanded them to stop. He also said the Lord would deliver Laban to them.

As soon as the angel left, Laman and Lemuel began to complain. Nephi and Sam had been beaten and ridiculed, but they did not react as their older brothers had. Nephi said, "Let us go up again unto Jerusalem, and let us be faithful in keeping the commandments of the Lord" (1 Nephi 3:16). Laman, Lemuel, Nephi, and Sam returned successfully to their father. (How they accomplished this is a story for another time.)

The Lord told Lehi that the brothers should once more return to Jerusalem. This time they were to bring some of their family friends back with them to the wilderness. Lehi told his family that the Lord wished Laman, Lemuel, Nephi, and Sam to have wives so their family could grow. Lehi's friend Ishmael and his family were chosen by the Lord to accompany them. Once again, the four brothers set off to Jerusalem.

They arrived at Ishmael's home and explained their purpose. Ishmael and his family agreed to journey with the young men. Along the journey, some of Ishmael's family rebelled with Laman and Lemuel. This group decided they preferred to return to Jerusalem. Nephi was "grieved for the hardness of their hearts" (1 Nephi 7:8). He spoke to them, saying,

> How is it that ye have not hearkened unto the word of the Lord?
>
> How is it that ye have forgotten that ye have seen an angel of the Lord?
>
> Yea, and how is it that ye have forgotten what great things the Lord hath done for us, in delivering us out of the hands of Laban, and also that we should obtain the record?
>
> Yea, and how is it that ye have forgotten that the Lord is able to do all things according to his will, for the children of men, if it so be that they exercise faith in him? Wherefore, let us be faithful to him. (vv. 9–12)

The group of dissenters heard Nephi and were angry. Laman, Lemuel, and two of the sons of Ishmael tied up Nephi and planned to leave him in the wilderness to be attacked by wild animals. Nephi prayed to the Lord that he could break the bands, and the Lord answered his prayer.

His brothers and the two sons of Ishmael again tried to bind Nephi, but one of the daughters of Ishmael, one of the sons of Ishmael, and their mother pled for Nephi's life. The four men agreed to let Nephi go. They even grew sorrowful for the things they had done to Nephi and asked his forgiveness. In his account, Nephi says, "And it came to pass that I did frankly forgive them all that they had done, and I did exhort them that they would pray unto the Lord their God for forgiveness. And it came to pass that they did so. And after they had done praying unto the Lord we did again travel on our journey towards the tent of our father" (1 Nephi 7:21).

Nephi struggled with his relationship with his two eldest brothers. They were rebellious when he was obedient. They were violent when he was peaceful. Yet through these hard times, Nephi's attitude never changed. He prayed for his brothers; he encouraged them to pray; he taught them the ways of the Lord; he freely forgave them when they hurt him. Nephi did all of these things with a spirit of love and patience. It is easy to be kind and patient to those who treat us similarly, but the Lord expects more.

He expects us to be patient with everyone, regardless of their actions toward us.

Journal Prompt: Often it is easier to be patient with the people outside our home than it is with our family members. Do you agree or disagree? Write about how Nephi was patient with his brothers. Record in your journal a plan to be more patient with your siblings, family members, and friends.

Activity: Think of someone whom you consider to be a patient person. Write a thank-you letter to this person explaining that when you think of patience you think of them, and tell them why.

8. Altruism

Definition: Selflessness; concern for the welfare of others.

Song: "Lord, I Would Follow Thee" (*Hymns,* 220)

Scriptures: John 13:34–35; 1 John 3:16–19; 1 John 4:21

The Sons of Mosiah
Mosiah 28

Mosiah was a Nephite king who had four sons, Ammon, Aaron, Omner, and Himni. These young men, along with Alma the Younger, persecuted members of the Church. Their actions caused their fathers much heartache.

Alma the Younger had an exciting and miraculous conversion experience that his friends witnessed. This event led to their own conversions to the gospel. As is the case with true conversion, the sons of Mosiah wanted to repair any wrongs they had committed. They now wished to share the joy they had discovered. "Now it came to pass that after the sons of Mosiah had done all these things, they took a small number with them and returned to their father, the king, and desired of him that he would grant unto them that they might, with these whom they had selected, go up to the land of Nephi that they might preach the things which they had heard, and that they might impart the word of God to their brethren, the Lamanites—that perhaps they might bring them to the knowledge of the Lord, their God" (Mosiah 28:1–2).

Despite the hatred of the Lamanites toward their people, these four brothers wanted nothing more than to share the gospel. In fact, "they were desirous that salvation should be declared to every creature, for they could not bear that any human soul should perish" (Mosiah 28:3). So sorry were they for the sinful lives they had lived that they wanted to live out the rest of their days in service to God and their fellow men. They knew that the Lamanites vowed to destroy their people, but they also knew that all men are children of God and need to hear His truth.

When the brothers returned to their father, they pleaded with him to allow them to travel to the land of Nephi, where the Lamanites were. King Mosiah prayed to the Lord, asking whether his sons should go preach to the Lamanites. The Lord told Mosiah to allow his sons to go. The Lord promised eternal life to the young men and assured Mosiah of their safe return.

Mosiah granted their request. He inquired of his people whom they would have the throne passed to since Mosiah was becoming an old man. The people announced Ammon as their choice. Ammon was given the opportunity to rule over all the land. His great desire, however, was to share the gospel with the Lamanites. He refused the throne, as did his three brothers.

They were given the chance to rule a kingdom. They had, within their grasp, all the worldly things they could want; instead they chose to follow Heavenly Father and to lead others to Him. They wanted to make amends for all of their wrong doings, not only to the people, but also to God.

Journal Prompt: Do you know someone who is serving a mission? What do you most admire about him or her? How does the story of the sons of Mosiah make you feel about the missionaries? How does it make you feel about serving a mission?

Activity: You can be a missionary like the sons of Mosiah. Write a family testimony on the inside covers of several copies of the Book of Mormon. Give them to people you know or meet. You might also give them to the missionaries to give out.

9. Diligence

Definition: Persistent application to an undertaking; steady effort.

Song: "Put Your Shoulder to the Wheel" (*Hymns,* 252)

Scriptures: Deuteronomy 6:17; Psalm 119:4; 2 Peter 3:14; Alma 17:2; D&C 58:26–28; D&C 107:99

The Parable of the Piece of Silver
Luke 15:8–10

Jesus was and is the greatest teacher of all time. The lessons He gave were often in story form, or parables. Many of the people He tried to instruct were those who felt they already knew the law.

The Pharisees were some of these people. The Pharisees were a religious party among the Jews. They prided themselves on their strict observance of the law. They took every opportunity to try to trick Jesus into saying things that were contrary to their beliefs. They not only thought they knew the commandments, but they also tried to persuade the people that Jesus was breaking their laws.

Jesus always humbly replied with the truth. On one occasion, Jesus had called to Him the sinners and publicans. The publicans were often the men employed by King Herod to collect taxes from the Jewish people. They were despised by the Jews. When Jesus summoned these people to join Him, the Pharisees were angry and complained that Jesus was eating with sinners. Instead of openly rebuking the Pharisees, Jesus chose to teach them using a parable.

The Savior said, "What woman having ten pieces of silver, if she lose one piece, doth not light a candle, and sweep the house, and seek diligently till she find it? And when she hath found it, she calleth her friends and her neighbours together, saying, Rejoice with me; for I have found the piece which I had lost. Likewise I say unto you, there is joy in the presence of the angels of God over one sinner that repenteth" (Luke 15:8–10).

There are two examples of diligence in this scripture story: one is the diligence of the woman in the parable who searched continually for the piece of silver. The other is the diligence shown by the Savior in instructing the people. Jesus never gave up on teaching the people around Him. He didn't allow prejudice or fear to stop Him, even though He was ridiculed and tortured. Jesus Christ's life and teachings show us the importance of every person to our Heavenly Father and His diligence in securing our return to His presence.

The parable of the piece of silver demonstrates the worth of souls. If Jesus is the woman who lost the coin and we are the silver, it is easy to see how He values us. And we are to follow His example. In this instance, we are to search for other pieces of silver and bring them to Christ. We have a huge responsibility to do missionary work. The Lord is counting on us to be diligent in this work by bringing people to Him.

In a revelation to the Prophet Joseph Smith, Oliver Cowdery, and David Whitmer, the Lord said,

> Remember the worth of souls is great in the sight of God;
>
> For behold, the Lord your Redeemer suffered death in the flesh; wherefore he suffered the pain of all men, that all men might repent and come unto him.
>
> And he hath risen again from the dead, that he might bring all men unto him, on conditions of repentance.
>
> And how great is his joy in the soul that repenteth!
>
> Wherefore, you are called to cry repentance unto this people.
>
> And if it so be that you should labor all your days in crying repentance unto this people, and bring, save it be one soul unto me, how great shall be your joy with him in the kingdom of my Father!
>
> And now, if your joy will be great with one soul that you have brought unto me into the kingdom of my Father, how great will be your joy if you should bring many souls unto me!" (D&C 18:10–16)

Journal Prompt: Write the definition of diligence in your journal. Think of one specific thing you would like to work on following through with diligently—for example, learning a new skill or game. Write a plan of how to accomplish this task and how you will stick with it.

Activity: One of the things the Lord has instructed us to do is to keep the Sabbath day holy. This is a commandment that requires diligence. The world in which we live is not always kind to our efforts to maintain this law and we must be conscientious because of this. To help your family find Sunday-appropriate activities on a regular basis, decorate a Sunday Box containing ideas for the Sabbath. You might include reading Church magazines, playing games that are suitable for Sunday, writing missionaries, and other quiet and uplifting activities.

10. Dedication

Definition: To devote oneself to a particular thought or action.

Song: "Seek the Lord Early" (*Children's Songbook*, 108)

Scriptures: Psalm 63:1; Isaiah 55:6; D&C 88:63

The Widow's Mites
Mark 12:13, 41–44

*O*n one of the many occasions that Jesus taught multitudes of people, Pharisees and Sadducees were gathered. These men tried, as always, to "catch him in his words" (Mark 12:13). They had already questioned Jesus on a number of issues.

After patiently dealing with these men, Jesus moved to sit near the treasury where money offerings were made. These offerings, sometimes called alms, were given by the people to help the poor. Jesus observed many people drop in money. He noticed that some of the rich put in quite a bit of money. He then drew the people's attention to a poor widow. This woman dropped in all her money, which was only two mites—a tiny sum.

Jesus called his disciples, saying, "Verily I say unto you, That this poor woman hath cast more in, than all they which have cast into the treasury: For all they did cast in of their abundance; but she of her want did cast in all that she had, even all her living" (Mark 12:43–44).

Have you ever heard the saying, "Give till it hurts"? That is what the widow did. It is admirable that so many people gave to the treasury, but

Jesus pointed this woman out as an example to His disciples. For her to give so much showed her dedication to the Lord. Giving of our substance, or tithing, is a commandment; but the decision to do this will show our dedication to the Lord. This is one of the many things about which we can be given personal revelation.

Journal Prompt: Do you agree that tithing isn't about money at all, but about faith? Why do you think the law of tithing is a commandment? In what other ways can we show our dedication to the gospel and other aspects of our life such as school or work?

Activity: Decorate jars for tithing and mission funds. You could write or print scriptures about tithing to glue on your jar.

11. Gentleness

Definition: Considerate, meek, mild, or kindly in disposition.

Song: "Each Life That Touches Ours for Good" (*Hymns,* 293)

Scriptures: D&C 19:23; Matthew 11:29; Galatians 5:22; 2 Timothy 2:24; James 3:17

Little Children to Come unto Jesus
Matthew 18:1–6; Luke: 18:15–17; 3 Nephi 17: 21–24

*J*esus' ministry included many miraculous events. He healed the sick, blind, lame, and deaf and raised people from the dead. Some of the most tender moments recorded about the Savior, however, are those with little children.

As Jesus was teaching a crowd, some of the people brought their children forward. They wanted Jesus to touch their children and bless them. The apostles tried to turn the people away, but Jesus stopped them. He said, "Suffer little children to come unto me, and forbid them not: for of such is the kingdom of God" (Luke 18:16). Jesus showed those around Him how precious little children are to our Father in Heaven.

The Savior taught an important lesson. "Verily I say unto you, Whosoever shall not receive the kingdom of God as a little child shall in no wise enter therein" (Luke 18:17). Children see things plainly, simply, and with great innocence. They tend to be kind, gentle, and obedient. Christ urges adults to emulate children in these precious qualities. The gospel is a beautiful gift from a loving Heavenly Father. As we embrace it with childlike faith, we are able to draw closer to our Savior.

On another occasion, the disciples asked Jesus who was the greatest in heaven. Jesus called forth a child. He put the child in the center of the disciples and said, "Verily I say unto you, Except ye be converted, and become as little children, ye shall not enter into the kingdom of heaven. Whosoever therefore shall humble himself as this little child, the same is greatest in the kingdom of heaven" (Matthew 18:3–4). This answer to the disciples gives insight into what is truly important to the Lord.

As King Benjamin said, "For the natural man is an enemy to God, and has been from the fall of Adam, and will be, forever and ever, unless he yields to the enticings of the Holy Spirit, and putteth off the natural man and becometh a saint through the atonement of Christ the Lord, and becometh as a child, submissive, meek, humble, patient, full of love, willing to submit to all things which the Lord seeth fit to inflict upon him, even as a child doth submit to his father" (Mosiah 3:19). Through the Atonement, we come closer to having those gentle, Christlike qualities.

Another moving example of Christ's gentleness occurred in the Americas. Jesus appeared to some 2,500 Nephites after His resurrection. He stayed with them many days, teaching, ministering, and calling disciples. Jesus Christ prayed for the Nephite people in their presence. He told them that they would be blessed for their faith, and He wept for them. Jesus then took their children, blessed each one, and prayed for them. Once more He shed tears. Jesus said, "Behold your little ones" (3 Nephi 17:23). The people saw the heavens open and angels descend from heaven. The angels made a circle around the children and ministered to them. It must have been amazing to behold.

These events illustrate the gentleness of the Savior. We have the obligation to learn from Christ and do as He did, being gentle with those we teach, serve, and live with.

Journal Prompt: How do you think it must have felt to be one of the children Jesus called to Him? How can you be more gentle with children, friends, family, or animals?

Activity: Draw a picture with a pencil of a scripture story displaying gentleness. Make them dot-to-dot by either erasing outside lines and replacing them with dots or putting a blank piece of paper on top of the drawing and putting the dots on the blank piece of paper. Photocopy the dot-to-dot pictures and give them to the nursery leaders to use in their classes.

12. Flexibility

Definition: Responsive to change; adaptable.

Song: "I Need Thee Every Hour" (*Hymns*, 98)

Scriptures: D&C 19:30; Psalm 18:2; Psalm 37:5

Feeding the Five Thousand
John 6:1–4

Jesus traveled across the Sea of Galilee and many people followed Him because they had heard of the many miracles our Savior had worked. The people were anxious to be close to Him and to see what mighty thing might happen next.

Jesus taught the people all day in a nice, grassy spot. As the afternoon wore on, the people became hungry. Jesus' disciples suggested they dismiss the people to go and get food. Jesus offered a different suggestion to His disciple Philip, "Whence shall we buy bread, that these may eat? And this he said to prove him: for he himself knew what he would do" (John 6:5–6). Philip responded that they could not afford to buy bread for all those who had gathered; even if they could purchase some, each person would get only a tiny morsel.

As the apostles pondered this, the Apostle Andrew approached Jesus with a young boy and told them the boy had five loaves of bread and two little fish that he was willing to share. "But what are they among so many?" Andrew asked (John 6:9). Jesus told his apostles to have all the people (about five thousand) sit down on the grass. Jesus took the bread from the boy and gave thanks for it. He gave it to his disciples and had them distribute it among the crowd. He then did the same thing with the fish. The scriptures tell us that when they were filled, the apostles gathered the remnants of the meal at Jesus' request. They gathered twelve baskets full of leftover bread after all had eaten. "Then those men, when they had seen the miracle that Jesus did, said, This is of a truth that prophet that should come into the world" (v. 14).

The scriptures tell us that not only was the multitude fed, but was also filled. This is a story that reminds us that, through faith in Jesus Christ, all things are possible. Our ideas may not always be His. The disciples had planned to send the people away for food—a very practical plan. However, Jesus "knew what he would do," and used this opportunity as a teaching moment (John 6:6). He taught His followers to be flexible. He taught them to see beyond what the world put in front of their eyes. He teaches us the same thing—we call it eternal perspective. It is important for us to remain flexible in seeing things of the Spirit and having the faith required to act upon those impressions.

Journal Prompt: Flexibility is being able to bend, or not be rigid. Think of clay. Isaiah said, "But now, O Lord, thou art our father; we are the clay, and thou our potter; and we all are the work of thy hand" (Isaiah 64:8). Being flexible in the Lord's hands means that we can be shaped into what He would have us be. We can be an instrument in His hands for good. Are you flexible for the Lord? Can you think of a time when you went (or tried to go) against the Lord?

Activity: Have a fish and bread meal with your family. If you have children who don't like fish, try fish sticks.

Breadsticks

1½ cups hot water	2 Tbsp. sugar
1 Tbsp. yeast	3 cups flour
1½ tsp. salt	

Preheat oven to 350 degrees. Mix water and sugar; cool to warm. Add yeast and let it activate. Add flour and salt. Mix and knead for about 3 minutes. Let rest for 10 minutes. Pull off 1-inch pieces of dough. Roll into breadsticks. (This may be a good time to remind your family about being flexible like the dough.) Dip these in butter and bake as is or twist two sticks together. Bake at 350 degrees for about 10 minutes or until golden brown.

13. Thankfulness

Definition: Grateful; acknowledgment of a favor.

Song: "God's Daily Care" (*Hymns,* 306)

Scriptures: Psalm 36:7; Psalm 68:19, Psalm 136:1–3; Colossians 3:15; Mosiah 7:12

Healing the Ten Lepers
Luke 17:11–19

Jesus traveled throughout the land on His mission to teach the gospel. He walked from town to town with the apostles. When they heard that Jesus was approaching, many people gathered in the streets to see, hear, or touch Him. News of the Savior's miracles spread quickly and the multitudes wanted to follow Him.

Jesus arrived in a particular village where He was greeted from afar by ten men. These men had been plagued with the terrible disease leprosy. These men wouldn't come closer to Jesus because they thought they were contagious. Immediately upon sighting Jesus, the men shouted out to Him, "Jesus, Master, have mercy on us" (Luke 17:13). These men had heard of the acts of the Savior and had great faith that He could heal them. Jesus called to the men to go and show themselves to their priests. The men walked away to do as they had been directed. Along the way, their illnesses were healed. "And *one* of them, when he saw that he was healed, turned back, and with a loud voice glorified God, And fell down on his face at his feet, giving him thanks" (vv. 15–16; emphasis added).

The story could have ended here, except for the word *one*. Only one man returned to thank the Savior and to glorify God. There were nine men healed, but only one thought to show gratitude for what had been given to him. Jesus said, "Were there not ten cleansed? but where are the nine?" (Luke 17:17). He continued, "There are not found that returned to give glory to God, save this stranger" (v. 18).

We are given many gifts from our Heavenly Father and His Son. If we were to pay attention, we would see that these blessings occur daily. We are cured of many afflictions through the love of our Savior. Our afflictions may not be a sickness or disease as in the case of the lepers, but we can feel the healing power of our Elder Brother in many aspects of our lives.

We have been healed of anger when we forgive; we have been healed of pride when we become humble. The list of weaknesses of man can be followed with a list of virtues we can attain if we ask for them and show thankfulness when He provides them. Instead of being one of the nine who didn't return to thank Jesus, we aspire to be that one that remembers what has been done for us and go to the Savior in thanks.

Journal Prompt: In your journal, list people you are thankful for and why you are thankful for them. Then write some of the things for which you are thankful. Remember to thank Heavenly Father for these people and things in your prayers.

Activity: Make thank-you cards using cardstock, construction paper, or scrapbooking paper. Choose someone from your list of people you are thankful for and show your thankfulness for that person in a thank-you card.

14. Consideration

Definition: Having regard for the needs or feelings of others; thoughtful.

Song: "Let Us Oft Speak Kind Words" (*Hymns,* 232)

Scriptures: Proverbs 16:24; Ephesians 4:29–32

Joseph Sees His Brothers Again
Genesis 39–45

Joseph had overcome many trials and was made a great ruler in Egypt by the pharaoh. His family thought he was dead.

Joseph had arrived in Egypt a slave. He was bought by a man named Potiphar, who noticed Joseph was a righteous young man. Potiphar made Joseph the overseer of his household. Potiphar's wife tried to seduce Joseph, saying, "Lie with me," but Joseph refused (Genesis 39:7). This angered Potiphar's wife, who told Potiphar that Joseph mocked her and had wanted to lay with her. Potiphar imprisoned Joseph.

While in jail, Joseph interpreted the dreams of some of the prisoners. Word reached the pharaoh that Joseph interpreted dreams. This interested the pharaoh because he had recently had a disturbing dream that he and his advisors couldn't quite figure out. So the pharaoh called for Joseph, who successfully explained the dream, gaining the pharaoh's respect and admiration in the process.

The dream was a message from Heavenly Father to prepare the people for a famine. For seven years the people would be able to harvest all of their crops to provide for themselves. After those seven years of abundance, though, there would follow seven years of famine.

Joseph said the Lord wanted the people to store all of the grains and other foods that they could in order to prepare for the seven years of famine. The pharaoh placed Joseph as his right-hand man to help in the next fourteen years. The people in Egypt followed Joseph's counsel and worked hard during the first seven years. Then came the seven years of "dearth," which means a scarcity, or a lack of something (Genesis 41:54). When the people had used up their personal stores, Joseph opened the storehouse and sold the corn.

Joseph's family also suffered from lack of food. Joseph's father, Jacob, heard there was corn for sale in Egypt. He sent his sons to purchase some, except Benjamin, the youngest, who stayed with his father. When the ten brothers arrived in Egypt, they bowed down before Joseph. They didn't recognize him as their brother, but Joseph knew them. He asked about his father and Benjamin. Joseph didn't know if his brothers were still the jealous brothers who had dealt so harshly with him in his youth, so he concocted a scheme to find out if their hearts had changed.

He accused them of being spies. He told them they could all go—except one. One brother would have to stay in prison until they brought back their younger brother. This, he said, would prove their honesty.

Now Joseph was speaking through an interpreter in a different language than his brothers. They thought Joseph could not understand their language, so they spoke with one another without fear of being discovered. The brothers began to sorrow about their predicament. They said this affliction was punishment for the terrible way they had treated their brother Joseph. Joseph realized they were truly repentant and had to turn away to hide his tears.

Joseph bound Simeon. He then sent the other brothers on their way. Joseph commanded his servants to load the brothers' sacks with the corn and to also place there the money they had brought for payment. On the way home, one of the brothers noticed that the money he had brought for payment was in his sack. He told his brothers, and they were afraid. Once they arrived home, they told their father, Jacob, all that had happened.

Jacob was concerned. He did not want Benjamin to go to Egypt because their family had already lost Joseph and now possibly Simeon. His sons convinced him they would look after Benjamin. Jacob finally consented and the brothers went to Egypt again. This time they were greeted by Joseph's servant, who led them into Joseph's home. They were given food and water and were told to wait. Joseph came in and inquired about his father. When he saw Benjamin, Joseph's emotions overcame him again and he had to leave quickly to avoid being seen crying. Once he had composed himself, Joseph returned and ate with his brothers.

When it was time to leave, Joseph asked his servant to fill each man's sack with grain and put his silver cup in Benjamin's sack. Joseph wanted to be sure of the intentions and virtues of his brothers. He told his servant to ride after the brothers and accuse one of stealing from Joseph, which was punishable by death. His servant obeyed and each brother emptied his sack. Of course the cup was found in Benjamin's sack. The brothers returned to the city. Instead of allowing his brother to be killed, Judah offered to take his brother's place. Judah spoke about all their father had been through in losing Joseph and the possibility of losing Benjamin. He could not hurt his father by letting Benjamin stay. He offered to stay as a slave if only Joseph would allow Benjamin to return home to his father.

Joseph saw the love his family had and could no longer keep his identity a secret. He revealed himself to them. He asked his brothers not to be upset for what they had done to him. He said, "God did send me before you to preserve you. . . . So now it was not you that sent me hither, but God: and he hath made me a father to Pharaoh, and lord of all his house, and a ruler throughout all the land of Egypt" (Genesis 45:7–8).

Joseph was not angry with his brothers. He did not want them to feel guilty. He knew that the Lord has a plan for all things. He was happy to be an instrument in the hands of his God. Joseph could have been vengeful towards his brothers, but he showed consideration for them. He opened his arms to embrace them and opened his heart to accept them.

Journal Prompt: After everything Joseph had been through—being sold into slavery by his brothers, false accusations, and imprisonment—it would have been reasonable for him to harbor ill feelings. Joseph, however, showed understanding, compassion, and consideration for his brothers and his father. How does this story of Joseph set an example for us to follow? How can you better implement this virtue in your life?

Activity: Is there a less-active family you could invite to your home for dinner and a family fireside? Perhaps there is a family in your ward that you would like to get to know better or someone you know who may be going through a hard time. Plan to do something for them.

15. Unity

Definition: Oneness.

Song: "Little Pioneer Children" (*Children's Songbook,* 216)

Scriptures: Mosiah 18:21; John 10:30; Psalm 133:1

Paul Counsels the Saints
Romans 15

After Jesus was resurrected, His disciples continued to travel throughout the land preaching and teaching the Savior's gospel. Paul counseled the early Saints often in the form of epistles. An epistle is often referred to as a letter, but the Bible Dictionary says, "An epistle in its best sense is more than a letter; it is a formal teaching instrument" ("Epistles," 667).

Paul based his teachings on what each audience needed. He continually affirmed the need for all Christians to be unified as the "body of Christ" (1 Corinthians 12:27). As part of a unified body, Paul encouraged the people to treat all people with kindness and love when he said, "We then that are strong ought to bear the infirmities of the weak, and not to please ourselves. Let every one of us please his neighbor for his good to edification. For even Christ pleased not himself" (Romans 15:1–3).

Paul further pled for unity when he told the people, "Now the God of patience and consolation grant you to be likeminded one toward another according to Christ Jesus: That ye may with one mind and one mouth glorify God, even the Father of our Lord Jesus Christ. Wherefore receive ye one another, as Christ also received us to the glory of God" (Romans 15:5–7).

Paul encouraged the people of his day to remain unified. That counsel does not change today. We are the body of Christ as members of His Church and should always "bear the infirmities of the weak" (Romans 15:1) and "receive . . . one another" (v. 7).

Journal Prompt: A unified family can help you fight against the negative influences of the world. How can you help your family be stronger? Write what you love about different members of your family and focus on those things. How does contention affect your family? What can you do to eliminate contention in your home?

Activity: Family unity is important. The family is central to Heavenly Father's plan of happiness. To encourage family unity, create a family notebook with pages for each child. Use the notebook to record personal interviews with each child in the family. Interview family members monthly. You can include personal testimonies, pictures of family members, family rules, talks or lessons given by family members in church, and so forth.

16. Meekness

Definition: Showing patience and humility; gentle; submissive to divine will.

Song: "Lord, We Come Before Thee Now" (*Hymns,* 162)

Scriptures: Deuteronomy 4:29; Ether 3:2

Jesus Suffers in Gethsemane
Luke 22:39–46

This is a story that would best be read directly from the scriptures and discussed as a family. Turn off any background noise (including the telephone), sit close together, read out loud, share your feelings, and pray.

Journal Prompt: Write your feelings about what happened in Gethsemane. How did Christ's meekness affect the Atonement? It has been said that we all face our own Gethsemane. What is a Gethsemane you are facing right now and how can meekness help you get through it? How would this make you feel closer to the Savior?

Activity: Write a poem or song or draw a picture to remind you of Christ's meekness. Put this in your Virtue Scrapbook.

17. Confidence

Definition: Trust or reliance.

Song: "Sing Praise to Him" (*Hymns,* 70)

Scriptures: Hebrews 10:35; D&C 17:1; D&C 121:45

A Woman Touches the Savior's Clothes
Mark 5:25–34

Wherever Jesus went preaching and teaching, people followed him. A woman who had been ill for twelve years was in the crowd one day. She had visited doctors, but instead of getting better, she grew worse. She heard about Jesus and knew that he could heal her, "For she said, If I may but touch his clothes, I shall be whole" (Mark 5:28). She approached the Savior and, reaching her hand through the crowds, touched the edge of His clothes. At once the woman's affliction left her and she was healed.

"And Jesus, immediately knowing in himself that virtue had gone out of him, turned him about in the press, and said, Who touched my clothes?" (Mark 5:30). The apostles marveled that Jesus could tell a certain individual had touched his clothing when so many people were around. Jesus looked around to find who had done this. The woman was afraid, but she came to Jesus and fell down at his feet, confessing. The Savior responded to this woman in a beautiful and loving way: "Daughter, thy faith hath made thee whole; go in peace, and be whole of thy plague" (v. 34).

Faith and confidence go hand in hand. Faith is a belief in things unseen. Like faith, confidence doesn't require a witness, but a trust in what we believe. This woman confidently came to the Savior because she knew He could cure her of the illness she had endured for so long. Her confidence was rewarded. Along with the joy of being healed, this woman experienced the approval and love of the Savior. We can experience the same happiness when we confidently show our faith in the Lord. It is humbling that we can please the Savior by having confidence and faith in Him.

Journal Prompt: Have you ever had a priesthood blessing when you were sick? The priesthood holders who give you a blessing have the authority to act in the name of Christ. Your blessings and healing came from the Savior, as the woman who touched his clothes experienced. How significant are blessings you have received? Have you had a special experience that increased your faith and confidence? Write about your experience.

Activity: Write a poem about having confidence in Jesus. Hang it with a picture of the Savior in your home.

18. Compassion

Definition: The deep feeling of sharing the suffering of another with the inclination to give aid or support or to show mercy.

Song: "Have I Done Any Good?" (*Hymns,* 223)

Scriptures: Zechariah 7:9; James 1:27

Baptisms at the Waters of Mormon
Mosiah 18

*I*n the land of Shilom, the wicked king Noah burdened his people with heavy taxes and used the money to fund his selfish desires. His priests were vain and prideful. He erected great buildings and decorated them with gold and silver. The Nephite people, under the rule of King Noah, fought off Lamanite attacks. Because of this, they became very prideful. They bragged about their strength and enjoyed wars.

The prophet Abinadi came among these unrighteous people and began to preach repentance. He boldly told King Noah and his priests of their sins. He encouraged them to give up their wicked ways and turn to the Lord for forgiveness. King Noah and his men were angered by Abinadi's warnings and had him imprisoned. Noah ordered Abinadi killed.

There was one man in the court of King Noah who was touched by the words of Abinadi. This man was Alma. He tried to convince King Noah to spare the prophet's life. Noah became angry with Alma, sent him away, and sent his men to slay him. Alma hid from the king's soldiers and wrote down the teachings of Abinadi. Alma repented of his sins and preached the things he had learned from Abinadi. He taught the people in secret so King Noah would not discover him and have him killed.

Alma found a secluded spot with an area of trees and a pool of water, called the Waters of Mormon, to hide during the day. The people came to this place to hear his teachings. "And he did teach them, and did preach unto them repentance, and redemption, and faith on the Lord" (Mosiah 18:7). Alma challenged them to be baptized. He said,

> As ye are desirous to come into the fold of God, and to be called his people, and are willing to bear one another's burdens, that they may be light;
>
> Yea and are willing to mourn with those that mourn; yea, and comfort those that stand in need of comfort, and to stand as witnesses of God at all times and in all things, and in all places that ye may be in, even until death, that ye may be redeemed of God, and be numbered with those of the first resurrection, that ye may have eternal life—
>
> Now I say unto you, if this be the desire of your hearts, what have you against being baptized in the name of the Lord, as a witness before him that ye have entered into a covenant with him, that ye will serve him and keep his commandments, that he may pour out his Spirit more abundantly upon you? (vv. 8–10)

The people were so excited about this challenge that they "clapped for joy, and exclaimed: This is the desire of our hearts" (v. 11). Alma gave special counsel about how to treat our fellow man with compassion. His words are part of the covenant, or promise, that we make as members of the Church. We promise to "bear one another's burdens, that they may be light" (Mosiah 18:8) and agree to "mourn with those that mourn; yea, and comfort those that stand in need of comfort" (v. 9). Whenever there is someone in need, we are to help them in any way we can. That may mean just giving somebody a hug or a smile. If we pray, Heavenly Father will show us how we can help those who need us. Compassion is what the Savior's life was all about. We promise to show it to our fellow man.

Journal Prompt: Write about your experience with the compassion activity. How does it make you feel to focus on the needs of others?

Activity: Discuss the need for compassion in our lives. Think of someone who stands in need of comfort. Perhaps he or she has lost a loved one or has been sick. Make something as a family to give to the person you have chosen. For example, you may want to make a dinner, dessert, or a card.

19. Trust

Definition: Confidence in the integrity, ability, character, and truth of a person or thing; to rely on.

Song: "I Need Thee Every Hour" (*Hymns,* 334)

Scriptures: 2 Samuel 22:3; Psalm 62:8; Hebrews 2:13; 2 Nephi 4:34

God Tries Abraham
Genesis 22

*A*braham was a prophet of God. He was an old man when the Lord told him that his wife, Sarah, was going to have a child. Sarah had waited many years for this joyful event. She gave birth to a son and named him Isaac because "he laugheth" (Bible Dictionary, "Isaac," 707). Sarah said, "God hath made me to laugh, so that all that hear will laugh with me" (Genesis 21:6). His birth was a miracle because Abraham was one hundred years old when Isaac was born.

When Isaac was just a boy, the Lord told Abraham to offer Isaac as a sacrifice to God. The law of sacrifice was important. The Bible Dictionary says that sacrifices "included offering the firstlings of their flocks in a similitude of the sacrifice that would be made of the Only Begotten Son of God. . . . This continued until the death of Jesus Christ, which ended the shedding of blood as a gospel ordinance" (Bible Dictionary, "Sacrifices," 765–766).

Abraham took Isaac and two servants and traveled three days to where the Lord wanted the sacrifice. He told his servants to stay behind while he and Isaac went to perform the sacrifice. Abraham and Isaac took wood and a knife and departed from the two men. As they went along, Isaac said to his father, "Behold the fire and the wood: but where is the lamb for the burnt offering?" (Genesis 22:7). Abraham responded, "My son, God will provide himself a lamb for a burnt offering" (v. 8).

Abraham built an altar where he had been instructed. He tied up Isaac and placed him on the altar. Imagine the trust Isaac had in his father, and the trust Abraham had in God!

Then Abraham drew out his knife and prepared to slay his precious son. At this moment, an angel spoke to Abraham saying, "Lay not thine hand upon the lad, neither do thou any thing unto him: for now I know that thou fearest God, seeing thou hast not withheld thy son, thine only son from me" (Genesis 22:12). As Abraham looked up, he saw a ram trapped in a nearby bush. Abraham took the ram and offered it as a burnt sacrifice in the place of Isaac. The Lord blessed Abraham for his faithfulness and trust.

We have trials in this life but the Lord has promised to strengthen us. When we put our trust in the Lord, He will help us through our trials. Heavenly Father wants to bless us; as we put our trust in Him, He will.

Journal Prompt: How do you think Abraham and Isaac felt during this trial? How does this scripture story make you feel about Abraham and Isaac? How do you think they developed their trust in the Lord? Do you think you would have enough faith and trust in such a trial? Why are you willing to trust certain people? Who do you know that is trustworthy?

Activity: Putting our trust in the Lord is one way of showing our love for Him. Have each family member pair up with another. Have one pair at a time stand facing the same direction. The person in front will be the "truster." He or she should take a giant step forward. On the count of three, the truster will fall backwards, keeping their legs straight. The person behind must catch the truster. Talk about how hard it was to let yourself go and trust the person to catch you. This is how it can be with trusting in Heavenly Father. We have to remind ourselves that He will not let us fall.

20. Service

Definition: An act to assist or benefit another.

Song: "Thy Spirit, Lord, Has Stirred Our Souls" (*Hymns,* 157)

Scriptures: Joshua 24:15; 2 Nephi 2:3; Mosiah 2:17; D&C 18:10–16

Jesus Washes the Disciples' Feet
John 13:1–17

Jesus gathered His twelve apostles together for a meal when He knew that His earthly mission was coming to an end. When all had eaten, Jesus brought out a basin of water and a towel. He told the disciples that He was going to wash their feet. Jesus had a great love for His twelve apostles. He "loved his own which were in the world, he loved them unto the end" (John 13:1). To show His love, He wanted to wash the apostles' feet as an act of service.

Jesus went from one man to another, washing and drying their feet. Peter told Jesus he wouldn't let Christ wash his feet. Jesus told him, "If I wash thee not, thou hast no part with me" (John 13:8). Peter consented, and Jesus finished His act of service.

Jesus sat with the apostles again and used this experience to teach a lesson. He said, "Know ye what I have done to you? Ye call me Master and Lord: and ye say well; for so I am. If I then, your Lord and Master, have washed your feet; ye also ought to wash one another's feet. For I have given you an example, that ye should do as I have done to you. Verily, verily I say unto you, The servant is not greater than his lord; neither he that is sent greater than he that sent him" (John 13:12–16).

The Savior's message is one of service. We are to serve one another just as He served the apostles, regardless of our social status. We are to serve those we love, and those in need. He truly is our example in all things.

Journal Prompt: Write your experiences after you do the activity below. Tell what you did and how it made you feel. Did serving others help you forget your own troubles? What would you like to do as a service for someone in your family? Set a goal to do an act of service every day.

Activity: Prayerfully choose a family service project. You might visit people in the hospital or a nursing home, invite an elderly person to your home for a meal, write to missionaries, or offer to babysit for a family with young children. Your family can do any little act of service to brighten the life of someone around you.

21. Courage

Definition: Bravery; the state or quality of mind that enables one to face danger with self-possession, confidence, and resolution.

Song: "Nephi's Courage" (*Children's Songbook,* 120)

Scriptures: Alma 24:19; Alma 48:13; 3 Nephi 6:20; Acts 4:13, 31

The Courage of Abinadi
Mosiah 11–17

*L*et's go back to the Americas 150 years before Christ was born. The king of the Nephites was a wicked man named Noah. King Noah sought to better himself and his closest friends. King Noah levied great taxes on his people and used the money to build an ornate palace. He had his throne and the seats of his priests made of the finest wood and covered in gold.

Meanwhile, the Lamanites continued attacking the Nephites. When the Nephites successfully drove away their enemies, they credited themselves and became prideful. The people no longer acknowledged the hand of God in their victories. They began to worship idols and to set their hearts on riches.

These were the conditions when Abinadi arrived in the land of Lehi-Nephi. Abinadi preached the gospel to Nephites who had fallen into an unrighteous way of life. He warned the people that unless they repented, the Lord would allow the Lamanites to conquer them. The people did not want to listen to Abinadi. They grew angry and tried to kill him, but the

Lord spared his life. King Noah heard about Abinadi and his prophecies concerning the destruction of the people. He was so angry that he ordered his subjects to find Abinadi so he could be executed.

Two years passed and no one had seen Abinadi. He disguised himself and prophesied of the bondage that awaited the Nephites should they continue to sin. He prophesied King Noah would be killed. The Nephites were furious. They tied up Abinadi and brought him before the king. They told Noah all that Abinadi had done and said, "And now, O king, behold we are guiltless, and thou, O king, hast not sinned; therefore, this man has lied concerning you, and he has prophesied in vain. And behold, we are strong, we shall not come into bondage, or be taken captive by our enemies" (Mosiah 12:14–15). King Noah threw Abinadi into prison. The king and his priests met together to determine Abinadi's fate. They decided to question him. To their surprise, Abinadi willingly and boldly answered their questions. The priests tried to confound Abinadi, but he only told them that they were "perverting the ways of the Lord" (v. 26).

King Noah grew angry with the prophet whom he declared to be mad, and he ordered his priests to kill Abinadi. As the priests approached him, Abinadi said, "Touch me not, for God shall smite you if ye lay your hands upon me, for I have not delivered the message which the Lord sent me to deliver; neither have I told you that which ye requested that I should tell; therefore God will not suffer that I shall be destroyed at this time. But I must fulfil the commandments wherewith God had commanded me; and because I have told you the truth ye are angry with me. And again, because I have spoken the word of God ye have judged me that I am mad" (Mosiah 13:3–4). The priests saw that Abinadi's face "shone with exceeding luster, even as Moses' did while in the mount of Sinai, while speaking with the Lord" (v. 5). They could not approach Abinadi as he began to speak.

Abinadi taught about the ten commandments, the Atonement, and many doctrines of the gospel. Abinadi then closed his prophecy by saying, "And now, ought ye not to tremble and repent of your sins, and remember that only in and through Christ ye can be saved? Therefore, if ye teach the law of Moses, also teach that it is a shadow of those things which are to come—Teach them that redemption cometh through Christ the Lord, who is the very Eternal Father" (Mosiah 16:13–15).

Alma, one of the king's priests, believed the words of Abinadi. He tried to convince the king to release Abinadi. King Noah threw Alma out of his court and sent his soldiers to kill him. Luckily, Alma escaped; but Abinadi was not as fortunate. The king ordered Abinadi to be bound and sent back to prison. After three days, Abinadi was brought before the king again. This time King Noah pronounced a sentence of death on Abinadi, unless he would deny all he had said. Abinadi answered him, saying, "I will not recall the words which I have spoken unto you concerning this people, for they are true; and that ye may know of their surety I have suffered myself that I have fallen into your hands. Yea, and I will suffer even until death, and I will not recall my words, and they shall stand as a testimony against you. And if ye slay me ye will shed innocent blood, and this shall also stand as a testimony against you at the last day" (Mosiah 17:9–10).

King Noah almost relented. He could sense the power of God in Abinadi and he was afraid. But the king's priests were cunning and reminded him that Abinadi had spoken out against him. King Noah allowed his anger to consume him. He ordered Abinadi's execution. Abinadi was bound with ropes and burned to death.

Abinadi never denied his words and never wavered in his faith. He told the king he was there to do the will of the Lord and would not leave until that was accomplished. He was true to his word and to his God.

Journal Prompt: The Lord can give us the strength and courage to face any trials. Have you ever been afraid of a new or strange situation? How does your faith in the Lord help you? What gave you courage?

Activity: As a family, list individual fears. Have a family "Face Your Fears Challenge." Brainstorm ways to help each other face fears. Give updates on each family member's progress in future family home evenings.

22. Joyfulness

Definition: A condition or feeling of great pleasure or happiness; delight.

Song: "Come, Rejoice" (*Hymns,* 9)

Scriptures: Luke 6:23; John 16:22; Galatians 5:22; D&C 128:19–21

Conversion of Alma the Younger
Mosiah 27:8–37

*A*lma the Younger had four friends who were the sons of King Mosiah. Alma's father was the high priest. These five boys, however, had not chosen to follow in their fathers' footsteps. Alma was a "very wicked and idolatrous man" who "led many people to do after the manner of his iniquity" (Mosiah 27:8). Alma and the sons of Mosiah persecuted the members of the Church. They tried to destroy the Church in secret. King Mosiah and the elder Alma prayed mightily for their children and for the members. King Mosiah had previously sent out a proclamation to all his subjects stating there was to be no persecution of any Church members, but the sons of Mosiah and Alma disregarded this decree. These five young men went about leading the weak astray and harassing those who would not join them—until an amazing thing happened.

An angel of the Lord descended from heaven right in front of Alma. All five young men fell to the ground in astonishment. The angel spoke, saying, "Alma, arise and stand forth, for why persecuteth thou the church of God?" (Mosiah 27:13). The angel continued, "Behold, the Lord hath heard the prayers of his people, and also the prayers of his servant, Alma, who is thy father; for he has prayed with much faith concerning thee that thou mightest be brought to a knowledge of the truth. . . . Alma, go thy way, and seek to destroy the church no more" (vv. 14–16). At this, Alma again fell to the ground. This time he was unable to stand back up. Alma could no longer speak, stand, or move his arms or legs. He had to be carried back to his father's house, where he remained in this state for three days and nights.

Alma later recounted his experience of what went on during those three days and nights. He said he was tormented by the thought of the sins he had committed in leading people astray. The tremendous weight of his wrongdoings tormented him "with all the pains of hell" (Alma 36:13). As Alma endured this agonizing torture of his soul, he recalled the words of his father. Alma the Elder had diligently testified to his son about Jesus Christ. He had prophesied of the Savior's coming and of the Atonement.

Alma recounts, "Now, as my mind caught hold upon this thought, I cried within my heart: O Jesus, thou Son of God, have mercy on me, who am in the gall of bitterness, and am encircled about by the everlasting chains of death" (Alma 36:18). Immediately after crying out this prayer in his heart, all of the agony Alma had thus suffered disappeared. He no longer felt the pain that had held him captive for three days and three nights.

Alma later exclaimed, "My soul was filled with joy as exceeding as was my pain! . . . There can be nothing so exquisite and sweet as was my joy" (Alma 36:20–21).

The joy that replaced Alma's pain was so powerful and beautiful that it sustained him the rest of his life. Alma experienced a great conversion of his heart. He repented of all he had done and turned completely away from the life he had lived. He became an instrument in the hands of the Lord. His joy truly was full.

Journal Prompt: How do you feel when you have done something you know to be wrong? How do you feel when you repent? Write in your journal as many things as you can think of that bring you personal joy. Now write about what you can do to bring joy to others.

Activity: Talk about what brings joy. Using photographs and pictures from magazines or newspapers, create a "Collage of Joy." Paste anything that makes family members feel joy.

23. Self-Discipline

Definition: To train, correct, and control oneself and one's conduct for improvement.

Song: "School Thy Feelings" (*Hymns,* 336)

Scriptures: Alma 38:12; Proverbs 16:32

The Parable of the Ten Virgins
Matthew 25:1–13

*M*any times Jesus taught lessons in parables. Sometimes He taught people who openly opposed Him. In this instance, Jesus was teaching His followers; therefore, it is of special interest to us.

A brief history of the customs of Israelite history may be helpful in understanding this parable. The Bible Dictionary states: "Among the Israelites, marriage was usually preceded by a formal act of betrothal, such a contract, when once entered on, being regarded as absolutely binding. On the marriage day, the bride was escorted to her husband's home by a procession consisting of her own companions and the 'friends of the bridegroom' or 'children of the bride-chamber,' some of them carrying torches, and others myrtle branches and chaplets of flowers. When she reached the house, words such as, 'Take her according to the law of Moses and of Israel' were spoken, the pair were crowned with garlands, and a marriage deed was signed. After the prescribed washing of hands and benediction, the marriage supper was held" ("Marriage," 728–29).

As with other parables, this lesson has symbolism. The bridegroom is

53

Jesus; the wedding feast is the coming of the Lord; and the ten virgins are His followers, including us.

The story begins with ten virgins, and "five of them were wise, and five were foolish." The first five were wise because they carried extra oil for their lamps with them to meet the bridegroom before the wedding feast. When there was no electricity, a lamp of oil was a very important thing. The five foolish virgins also carried their lamps, but because they anticipated the bridegroom's quick arrival, they brought no extra oil.

The bridegroom did not immediately greet the ten virgins; instead, he tarried. In other words, he delayed or took his time in coming. While the young women waited, they fell asleep. At midnight someone called out that the bridegroom was coming. The ten virgins were stirred from their slumber, and began to prepare. The five wise virgins trimmed their lamps (the wicks) and stood ready to meet the bridegroom. The five foolish virgins awakened, only to realize that their lamps had all but burned out. In a panic, they asked the other young women for oil to fill their lamps. The wise virgins told the foolish girls to go and buy oil for themselves, since they had only enough for their own lamps.

The foolish young women departed. While they were gone, the bridegroom arrived. The wise virgins were able to go in to the feast with him. Meanwhile, the foolish young women returned and found the door shut. They knocked on the door and asked to be let in. The bridegroom answered them by saying that he did not know them.

Our Savior ended this parable by saying, "Watch therefore, for ye know neither the day nor the hour wherein the Son of man cometh" (Matthew 25:13). Jesus' own people did not know when He came. They had watched and waited for signs of His coming. However, He walked among them and most still did not see.

Today we await the Second Coming of the Lord. We must discipline ourselves to stay in tune with the Spirit and keep our lamps full. We can do so when we follow the prophet, study the scriptures, pray, have family home evening, partake of the sacrament, and obey the commandments of God. Through self-discipline, we will be prepared to meet the bridegroom, our Savior, Jesus Christ.

Journal Prompt: What are some ways you can teach yourself discipline? Why is it important to do it on your own? Make a list of ways you can "fill your lamp" and commit to being prepared to meet Jesus. How do you think you will feel on that glorious day?

Activity: After reading the parable of the ten virgins, talk about the importance of preparedness for disasters and disaster plans in your area. As an alternate activity, make lamps out of clay or playdough to represent the scripture story. You can use a commercial clay or try the following recipe:

Salt Dough

1 cup salt
1¼ cups warm water
3 cups flour
acrylic paint

Mix ingredients together. Shape into lamps. Bake at 200 degrees until clay hardens and is slightly brown. The baking time will depend on how thick your sculptures are. Make sure it doesn't burn. After your lamps have dried, you can paint them.

24. Benevolence

Definition: An inclination or tendency to do kind or charitable acts.

Song: "All Things Bright and Beautiful" (*Children's Songbook,* 231)

Scriptures: D&C 6:33; Luke 6:27–35; 1 Timothy 6:18

The Creation
Genesis 1–2; Moses 1–3

We are all children of our Heavenly Father. We have been created in His image and have been placed here on this earth to learn and grow. Our Father loves us so much that He gave us this beautiful earth and everything on it.

"In the beginning God created the heaven and the earth" (Genesis 1:1). On this first day of creation, Jesus Christ (under the direction of Heavenly Father) separated the night from the day; darkness from light.

The second day dawned and God said, "Let there be a firmament in the midst of the water, and it was so, even as I spake; and I said: Let it divide the waters from the waters; and it was done; And I, God, made the firmament and divided the waters, yea, the great waters under the firmament from the waters which were above the firmament, and it was so even as I spake. And I, God, called the firmament Heaven; and the evening and the morning were the second day" (Moses 2:6–7).

Day three began with separating dry land with oceans. The dry land would be called earth, the waters called the sea. The earth was made to produce seeds, grass, trees, and all greenery.

The fourth day of creation involved the stars, sun, and moon. "And I, God, said: Let there be lights in the firmament of the heaven, to divide the day from the night, and let them be for signs, and for seasons, and for days, and for years; And let them be for lights in the firmament of the heaven to give light upon the earth; and it was so. And I, God, made two great lights; the greater light to rule the day, and the lesser light to rule the night, and the greater light was the sun, and the lesser light was the moon; and the stars also were made according to my word" (Moses 2:14–16.)

On the fifth day, God created all the animals of the sea and the birds in the air. He created dolphins, whales, sharks, fish, eagles, robins, owls, crows, and all the other sea and air creatures.

The sixth day of creation must have been a busy one. This is the day God populated the earth with land animals. We could not begin to name them all, even if we were to try. Every year new species are discovered, but Heavenly Father knows them all because He created them all. Next came a special part of creation: man.

> And I, God, said unto mine Only Begotten, which was with me from the beginning: Let us make man in our image, after our likeness; and it was so. And I, God, said: Let them have dominion over the fishes of the sea, and over the fowl of the air, and over the cattle, and over all the earth, and over every creeping thing that creepeth upon the earth.
>
> And I, God, created man in mine own image, in the image of mine Only Begotten created I him; male and female created I them. (Moses 2:26–27)

Heavenly Father created the Garden in Eden where the first man and woman, Adam and Eve, could dwell. Eden was a place of perfect beauty and peace. This was a gift from our Father. Heavenly Father knew that Adam must fall for the plan of salvation to continue, but this earth that we live on is still His gift to us. It was the first of many countless acts of benevolence and love that our Father has granted us. He has blessed us with life and all that comes with it. What we do with that life can be our gift to Him.

Journal Prompt: Have you ever considered the beauty in creation? All around you, no matter where you live, is evidence of Heavenly Father's love. You may see it in a bird's nest, in a gentle breeze, or in the blooming flowers. Write about your feelings of when you see beauty in nature, and think of the benevolence of Heavenly Father.

Activity: Take time daily to notice nature. Take a magnifying glass outside and sketch the things you see, paying attention to details. Collect leaves, flowers, or grass to press and dry in your Virtue Scrapbook. Photograph sunsets and landscapes. You will begin to discover things around you that you never even knew were there. Thank Heavenly Father for all that He has blessed us with on this earth.

25. Cheerfulness

Definition: Being in good spirits; happy.

Song: "Scatter Sunshine" (*Hymns*, 230)

Scriptures: Psalm 100:2; John 16:33; D&C 68:6

"The Lord Is My Shepherd"
Psalm 23

David was a young shepherd boy born more than a thousand years before Christ. His life began very simply. He tended sheep, played the harp, and sang songs of praise to God known as psalms. The Bible Dictionary says psalms are called " 'praises' in Hebrew but the word *mizmor*, which denotes a composition set to music, is found in the titles of many of them" ("Psalms," 754). Many of the Psalms were originally intended to have accompanying music or to be sung.

The twenty-third Psalm contains the imagery of a young shepherd. David cheerfully ascribes all goodness in his life to God. He sings of the mercy and comfort that come from our Heavenly Father.

As a family, read this Psalm verse by verse. Discuss the picture of cheerfulness David painted in each one.

> The Lord is my shepherd; I shall not want.
> He maketh me to lie down in green pastures: he leadeth me beside the still waters.
> He restoreth my soul: he leadeth me in the paths of righteousness for his name's sake.

Yea, though I walk through the valley of the shadow of death, I will fear no evil: for thou art with me; thy rod and thy staff they comfort me.

Thou preparest a table before me in the presence of mine enemies: thou annointest my head with oil; my cup runneth over.

Surely goodness and mercy shall follow me all the days of my life: and I will dwell in the house of the Lord for ever. (Psalm 23)

Journal Prompt: David's life may have started out simply, but it ended as anything but simple. The shepherd boy grew into Israel's greatest king. David passed through terrible trials in his life. How do you think the cheerful outlook he wrote of in the twenty-third Psalm served him throughout his life? How could that kind of attitude help you?

Activity: Try to put David's psalm to music and sing and play it as a family band. You can use instruments you already have or get creative and make your own instruments from household items.

26. Purity

Definition: Innocence; chastity; free from dirt, defilement, pollution, or guilt.

Song: "As Zion's Youth in Latter Days" (*Hymns*, 256)

Scriptures: D&C 97:21; Proverbs 15:26; Isaiah 52:11

Daniel
Daniel 1

Roughly six hundred years before Christ was born, a king named Nebuchadnezzar ruled Babylon. He attacked Jerusalem and brought back captives to his land. Among these prisoners was a young man named Daniel and his three friends Hananiah, Mishael, and Azariah.

Babylonian law was very different from the Mosaic law that these boys were familiar with. The Mosaic laws were very strict. The people were given very specific guidelines concerning nearly every aspect of their lives. One of those guidelines had to do with their food. The Lord told Moses exactly what the Israelites could and could not eat, how the food was to be prepared, and even who could prepare it. The faithful took these laws seriously. Read Leviticus 11 to see just how specific these laws were.

The king had the young Hebrew captives brought to the palace to be taught in the Chaldean customs. At this time, the Chaldeans were a learned class who studied astrology. Daniel and his friends were chosen for their health and strength and because they were "skillful in all wisdom, and cunning in knowledge, and understanding science" (Daniel 1:4).

They were given new names and were provided for by the king while they were instructed and trained in Babylonian ways.

As an Israelite, Daniel refused to break the Mosaic law. He would not partake of the food that was served. "But Daniel purposed in his heart that he would not defile himself with the portion of the king's meat, nor with the wine which he drank" (Daniel 1:8). Daniel went to his leader, Melzar, and made his feelings known. Melzar told Daniel that if he didn't eat he would grow weak and look sickly, and the king might blame Melzar. Daniel proposed that he and his Hebrew friends be given grains to eat and water to drink. After ten days, Melzar could compare Daniel and his friends to the young men eating the king's food. Melzar agreed. "And at the end of ten days their countenances appeared fairer and fatter in flesh than all the children which did eat the portion of the king's meat" (v. 15). From that time forward, Melzar replaced the king's meat with grains for the other Israelite children.

We no longer live by Mosaic law because Jesus Christ fulfilled that law and replaced it with a higher one. We do, however, have a guideline for keeping our bodies pure and healthy. It is called the Word of Wisdom. Within the Word of Wisdom are recommendations for healthy eating. Joseph Smith received this revelation on February 27, 1833; it says, in part, "All wholesome herbs God hath ordained for the constitution, nature, and use of man—Every herb in the season thereof, and every fruit in the season thereof; all these to be used with prudence and thanksgiving. Yea, flesh also of beasts and of the fowls of the air, I, the Lord have ordained for the use of man with thanksgiving; nevertheless they are to be used sparingly" (D&C 89:10–12). The Lord also said that grains are to be "the staff of life" (v. 14). There is a reason we are to eat these healthy foods. The apostle Paul said, "Know ye not that ye are the temple of God, and that the Spirit of God dwelleth in you?" (1 Corinthians 3:16). In order to keep our bodies pure, we need to put good foods into them and avoid harmful substances. When we do this, the Lord promises us blessings of health and strength.

Journal Prompt: Read the entire Word of Wisdom found in Doctrine and Covenants 89. Do you feel more clean or pure when you follow the Word of Wisdom? What blessings does the Lord promise if we follow His instructions?

Activity: As a family, try sprouting seeds such as clover or alfalfa. Place a few tablespoons of seeds in the bottom of a jar. Put in enough water to moisten the seeds, then drain off the rest. Place some mesh (you can cut off the toe part of panty hose) over the top of the jar to allow air to circulate. Roll the jar around so the seeds stick to the sides. Lay the jar on its side and watch for sprouts. After just a few days, you can use the sprouts in sandwiches or salads. If your seeds don't look very green, you can put them on a paper towel in the sun for a few minutes to brighten them up, but they can be eaten either way.

27. Faithfulness

Definition: Adhering firmly and devotedly, as to a person, cause, or ideal; loyalty; fidelity.

Song: "Faith" (*Children's Songbook,* 96)

Scriptures: Hebrews 11:1; Alma 32:28, 42–43; D&C 98:12, D&C 124:55, 113

Faith of the Israelites
Deuteronomy 6:5–9

The Lord delivered the Israelites from their bondage in Egypt. Moses led the people across the Red Sea on dry ground, and many miracles were performed for their sake as they traveled to the promised land.

The Israelites were led by the Lord in a pillar of cloud by day and a pillar of fire by night. When they complained about a lack of food, the Lord sent manna from heaven every day except the Sabbath for forty years. When the people needed water, Moses hit a rock with his staff and water came pouring out. When the Israelites were attacked, Moses stood on a hill with his staff raised above his head and his people began to conquer. When he dropped the staff, the Israelites started to lose the battle. Moses stood for so long with his staff raised that he grew weary. Some of his counselors sat Moses on a rock and held up his hands until the fighting was over. Moses was given detailed instruction on how to build a tabernacle, a sort of traveling temple, for the people while they wandered in the wilderness. He was called by the Lord to come to the top of Mt.

Sinai. Moses saw God and talked with Him face-to-face. It was there that the Lord gave Moses the Ten Commandments and had him write them on stone tablets. Moses came down from the mountain forty days later, and his skin shone so brightly from beholding the glory of God that even his brother and his counselors were afraid to come near him. They put a veil over his face while he spoke to them.

All of these amazing miracles and more happened to the Israelites during their exodus from Egypt. Sometimes the people were disobedient to the commandments they had been given. At times the people got caught up in their present circumstances and forgot their many blessings. Moses would then recount their experiences to remind them of how good the Lord had been.

Moses urged his people to follow the commandments and to teach them to their children. That way, Moses said, they could follow God wherever they were and pass the words of God down from generation to generation. He told them that if they obeyed the commandments they would receive the Lord's blessings. They would become a mighty people and would be given a promised land because of their faithfulness.

Moses told the Israelites that their God was the one true God. He said, "And thou shalt love the Lord thy God with all thine heart, and with all thy soul, and with all thy might" (Deuteronomy 6:5). Moses told the people to keep these words in their hearts. He also said, "And thou shalt teach them diligently unto thy children, and shalt talk of them when thou sittest in thine house, and when thou walkest in the way, and when thou liest down, and when thou risest up. And thou shalt bind them for a sign upon thine hand, and they shall be as frontlets [phylacteries] between thine eyes. And thou shalt write them upon the posts of thy house, and on thy gates" (vv. 7–9).

Moses was referring to the ancient Hebrew traditions behind phylacteries and mezuzot. The Bible Dictionary explains these interesting objects. Phylacteries are "amulets fastened on the forehead, or on the left arm. They were small strips of parchment inscribed with texts" ("Phylacteries," 751). Mezuzot are "passages of the law written on tiny scrolls, enclosed in a small container and nailed to the right door post or gate, as an ordinance of remembrance" (Deuteronomy 6:9, footnote a). These were outward signs of the ancient Hebrew's faithfulness and remembrance of the goodness of God.

The scriptures written on the phylacteries and mezuzot would have been commandments that the people were supposed to literally hold close to themselves. Moses was encouraging the Israelites to remember their God and to stay faithful. Jesus said the same to those He was teaching when He said, "Thou shalt love the Lord thy God with all thy heart, and with all thy soul, and with all thy mind. This is the first and greatest commandment" (Matthew 22:37–38). We were given an additional part by our Savior when He said, "And the second is like unto it, Thou shalt love thy neighbor as thyself. On these two commandments hang all the law and the prophets" (Matthew 22:39–40).

The words of Moses and of Jesus Christ tell us the same thing: we are to prove faithful to our God by being obedient to His laws. By keeping these commandments in our hearts and in our minds at all times. If we obey Him, the Lord will bless us.

Journal Prompt: How do you think the Israelites started forgetting their blessings? What helps you remember to stay faithful and remember the Lord's blessings?

Activity: Make a sign that contains Matthew 22:37–40. Write, paint, or use stickers on wood, paper, ceramic tile, or other writable surfaces. Display your sign in your home as your version of a mezuzot.

28. Selflessness

Definition: Altruistic; unselfish.

Song: "Love One Another" (*Children's Songbook,* 136)

Scriptures: John 13:34–35; John 15:13; 1 John 4:11

Baby Moses
Exodus 1 and 2

In the land of Egypt, a baby was born under the same kind of ruthless leader as was our Savior. The pharaoh of Egypt was concerned that the Hebrew population was growing at too fast a rate. He was afraid they would grow strong enough to overthrow his authority. The pharaoh's answer to this dilemma was alarming. He called the midwives of the Hebrew women together and told them to kill any male babies that were born. But the midwives were righteous and did not do as the pharaoh had ordered. He questioned the midwives about their disobedience. They told him the Hebrew women were strong and had delivered their babies on their own before the midwives could even arrive. Pharaoh then ordered all his people to drown any Hebrew baby boys.

During this tragic time, a Hebrew husband and wife had a baby boy. The baby's mother hid him for three months, but it became obvious that she could not keep him hidden forever. In a selfless act of love, she made a small basket for the baby and placed him in it among the reeds at the edge of the Nile River.

The baby's little boat rested in the reeds until he was discovered by none other than the pharaoh's daughter, who had come down to the river to bathe. She opened up the basket and saw the tiny bundle inside. One of her maidens, who happened to be the baby's sister, offered to go and find a Hebrew nurse to tend the baby. The pharaoh's daughter agreed, and the girl brought back her mother.

Pharaoh's daughter told the baby's mother that she could work as the nurse for the child. The new nurse took her baby and raised him as the son of Pharaoh's daughter. This little baby was called Moses, which means "to draw out," because he was drawn from the water (Exodus 2:10, footnote b).

Moses' mother made the difficult choice to give up her son in order to spare his life. She put aside her own feelings and did what was right for her child. We are given frequent opportunities to perform acts of selfless service. They may not always seem dramatic to us, but they may touch the lives of others in ways we may never fully know. Our Savior lived a life of selflessness and He invites us to follow His example.

Journal Prompt: How do you think putting others before ourselves could affect the decisions we make? What can you do to live a more selfless life?

Activity: Make a list of Church members who might need a ride to sacrament meeting. Invite them to ride with you. Invite someone who sits alone at church to sit with you.

29. Wisdom

Definition: Understanding what is true, right, or lasting; common sense; good judgment.

Song: "Search, Ponder, and Pray" (*Children's Songbook,* 109)

Scriptures: 2 Nephi 4:15; Jacob 6:11–12; Moroni 10:4–5

King Solomon
1 Kings 3–4

Solomon was the son of King David. He was only about twenty years old when he began to rule the vast empire (see Bible Map 4: The Empire of David and Solomon). Solomon loved the Lord and wanted to lead his people in a way that was pleasing to God.

One night, the Lord spoke to Solomon in a dream, asking him about his desires. Solomon said he felt that he was unable, on his own, to lead the people. He told God that he was "but a little child" (1 Kings 3:7). Solomon asked, "Give therefore thy servant an understanding heart to judge thy people, that I may discern between good and bad: for who is able to judge this thy so great a people?" (1 Kings 3:9).

The Lord was pleased that Solomon had not asked for riches or for revenge on his enemies. He said, "Behold, I have done according to thy words: lo, I have given thee a wise and an understanding heart; so that there was none like thee before thee, neither after thee shall any arise like unto thee" (1 Kings 3:12).

This wisdom and discernment that Solomon had been granted was soon evident. The custom of the day was to bring disputes before the king to be judged. Two women came to King Solomon with a dispute. Both women lived in the same home and each had recently given birth to a baby boy. One of the women said that in the night the other woman rolled over on her own child and the baby died. She said the woman then took the dead child and placed it by this woman's side and took the living baby as her own. The other woman objected, saying that it was the first woman whose child had died and who had swapped the babies.

King Solomon had to determine which of the women was the mother of the living child. He asked that a sword be brought to him. Solomon said, "Divide the living child in two, and give half to the one, and half to the other" (1 Kings 3:25).

One woman cried out, "O my lord, give her the living child, and in no wise slay it" (1 Kings 3:26).

The other woman said, "Let it be neither mine nor thine, but divide it" (1 Kings 3:36). Which woman do you suppose was the real mother? Solomon came to the same conclusion.

The scriptures say, "And God gave Solomon wisdom and understanding exceeding much, and largeness of heart, even as the sand that is on the sea shore" (1 Kings 4:29). Wisdom and understanding were and are important attributes in the sight of God. The Lord was happy Solomon chose to ask for these things when he could have requested anything. Heavenly Father's desire that we have wisdom did not end in the days of Solomon. In 1832 Joseph Smith revealed the Lord's counsel: "And as all have not faith, seek ye diligently and teach one another words of wisdom; yea, seek ye out of the best books words of wisdom; seek learning, even by study and also by faith" (D&C 88:118). Joseph was later instructed that "if a person gains more knowledge and intelligence in this life through his diligence and obedience than another, he will have so much the advantage in the world to come" (D&C 130:19).

President Gordon B. Hinckley counseled the youth: "The Lord wants you to educate your minds and hands, whatever your chosen field. . . . Seek for the best schooling available. Become a workman of integrity in the world that lies ahead of you. I repeat, you will bring honor to the Church and you will be generously blessed because of that training."[1] The Lord has given us a challenge to strengthen our minds and gain wisdom. He has also given us the formula for gaining wisdom: pray for wisdom and understanding, actively seek wisdom through the best books we can find, have faith in the Lord's desire to help us learn, and work hard in our schooling. Then we can enjoy the Lord's promised blessings of increased knowledge and understanding.

Journal Prompt: What do you most like learning about? What are your future plans? How will an education help you in those plans?

Activity: Have a "family share night." Let each person in the family teach others something. For little ones, it might be something as simple as how to make a PB&J sandwich. Maybe children could teach something they learned in school. The point is to share wisdom they have gained.

Notes

1. *New Era*, January 2001, 4.

30. Bravery

Definition: Possessing or displaying courage; valiant.

Song: "Hope of Israel" (*Hymns,* 259)

Scriptures: Ephesians 6:10–18; 2 Nephi 28:7–8, 20–28

Queen Esther
Esther 1–7

About five hundred years before Christ was born, there lived a king named Ahasuerus who ruled Persia and Media (see Bible Map 7: The Persion Empire). Ahasuerus held a great feast at his palace in Shushan. The festivities had gone on 180 days when Ahasuerus decided to call in his wife, Vashti, to show off her beauty to all the princes. Vashti refused to come before the king. Ahasuerus was furious with his wife for disobeying him. His princes and counselors suggested when the people heard about this incident, they might feel that the king's authority had been undermined. The counselors and princes feared women throughout the kingdom would begin disregarding their husbands' wishes. Ahasuerus decided to dethrone Vashti and choose a new queen.

The king ordered officers from each of his provinces to bring eligible young women to the palace. Mordecai, a Jewish man, heard the announcement and brought his niece, Esther, to the palace. Mordecai warned Esther not to divulge her religion. There was much persecution against the Jews at this time. Esther appeared before Ahasuerus and found favor with him. She was chosen to be the new queen.

Mordecai was working in Ahasuerus's palace when he discovered a plot to kill the king by two of the king's servants. Mordecai alerted Esther, who then notified Ahasuerus in Mordecai's behalf. The two men were hung, and the whole incident was recorded in the king's book of chronicles. Remember this, it will be important later!

Ahasuerus promoted a man from his court named Haman to the position of chief minister. Haman hated the Jewish people and wished to destroy them. The people had been commanded to bow to Haman, but Mordecai refused. Since Mordecai was Jewish, Haman decided to take this opportunity to get rid of Mordecai and his people. Haman went before the king to tell him that there was a group of people who refused to keep the king's laws but had laws of their own. Haman asked the king to let him decree that these people should all be killed. The king gave his permission for Haman to "do with them as it seemeth good to thee" (Esther 3:11). Haman sent a proclamation to every province in the kingdom "to destroy, to kill, and to cause to perish, all Jews, both young and old, little children and women, in one day, even upon the thirteenth day of the month" (v. 13). Mordecai and all the other Jewish people in Persia mourned.

Mordecai sent word to Esther telling her of the king's decree. Mordecai encouraged her to go before Ahasuerus, tell him of her heritage, and plead with him for the lives of her people. This was no easy task because in those days no one, not even the queen herself, was allowed to speak to the king without first being summoned by him. The law stated that if someone presented themselves unbidden before the king, he could be put to death. If, however, the king held out his golden scepter, the person's life would be spared. Esther responded to Mordecai's request by telling him that she was too frightened to go in to see the king. Mordecai reminded Esther that she, too, was Jewish, and that she would not escape the decree. He then encouraged her again by saying, "Who knoweth whether thou art come to the kingdom for such a time as this?" (Esther 4:14).

Esther sent an answer back to Mordecai that said, "Go, gather together all the Jews that are present in Shushan, and fast ye for me, and neither eat nor drink three days, night or day: I also and my maidens will fast likewise; and so will I go in unto the king, which is not according to the law: and if I perish, I perish" (Esther 4:16).

On the third day, Esther went into the king's chamber and stood waiting at the back wall. The king was happy to see Esther. He held out his scepter and the queen came forward. He asked Esther what she wished. He told her that he would give her anything, even half his kingdom. Esther said she only wanted Ahasuerus and Haman to come to a banquet she had prepared for them. The king agreed and summoned Haman. At the banquet, the king once again asked Esther what she desired. Esther invited both men to another banquet the following day. The king agreed and Esther made her preparations.

Haman was very pleased with what he thought was his good standing with the king and queen. As he departed from Esther's banquet, Haman noticed Mordecai at the king's gate. He remembered his wrath against the Jewish man who would not bow to him. Haman told his close friends and his wife that only Mordecai stood in the way of his happiness. He simply could not allow such disrespect. Haman's friends encouraged him to build a gallows upon which he could hang Mordecai for refusing to pay tribute to him. Haman ordered the gallows built and put Mordecai from his mind.

As Haman was planning Mordecai's death, the king lay in his bed unable to sleep. He called for his servant to bring him the book of chronicles that contained the records of events in the royal court. Ahasuerus read over the book and noted that Mordecai had saved his life by alerting him to the plot of his two household servants. He realized that no honor had been given Mordecai for his bravery. The king called Haman into his chamber. He asked Haman what should be done to recognize a loyal and honorable man. Haman thought, "To whom would the king delight to do honour more than to myself?" (Esther 6:6). Haman urged the king to heap honors on the man. He suggested that "the royal apparel be brought which the king useth to wear, and the horse that the king rideth upon, and the crown royal which is set upon his head: And let this apparel and horse be delivered to the hand of one of the king's most noble princes, that they may array the man withal whom the king delighteth to honour, and bring him on horseback through the street of the city, and proclaim before him, Thus shall it be done to the man whom the king delighteth to honour" (Esther 6:8–9).

The king told Haman to proceed with the honors; but to present them to Mordecai. Haman was obedient to the king. He did for Mordecai all he had suggested for himself and returned to his home to mourn. While there, Haman was summoned to Esther's banquet.

For the third time Ahasuerus offered Esther whatever her heart might desire. Esther told her husband that her life and the lives of her people were at stake. She announced that there was a man who wished to destroy her and her people. Ahasuerus was enraged. He demanded to know the identity of the culprit. Esther named Haman as the organizer of the scheme to wipe out all the Jewish community in Persia. Ahasuerus ordered Haman to be hanged on his own gallows.

Esther pleaded with the king to reverse the decree to destroy every Jew in the kingdom. Ahasuerus sent word across all Persia that no harm should come to Esther's people. Esther stood up for her people even in the face of death; the Jewish people were safe because of the bravery of one woman. We may not be called upon to make such a dramatic choice, but we have the opportunity to bravely stand as witnesses of Christ.

Journal Prompt: Have you ever been fearful about confronting something frightening? Just because you are afraid doesn't mean you aren't brave. Esther first told Mordecai that she wasn't sure she could face the king. What made her brave wasn't lack of fear. How do you think Esther demonstrated bravery?

Activity: Using butcher paper and two sticks or dowels, make a scroll by taping or gluing the ends of the paper to the sticks or dowels. Write the story of Esther on the scroll.

31. Dependability

Definition: Capable of being depended on; trustworthy.

Song: "I Will Be Valiant" (*Children's Songbook*, 162)

Scriptures: Alma 53:20–21

Helaman's Stripling Warriors
Alma 56–57

*A*mmon, one of the sons of Mosiah, was successful in spreading the gospel among the Lamanites. He and his brothers had been given permission by the king to preach throughout the land. The king sent word that none of these men were to be harmed. Through the sons of Mosiah "thousands were brought to the knowledge of the Lord" (Alma 23:5). These converted Lamanites had such a change of heart that they no longer wanted to be associated with the name Lamanite, so they began to call themselves Anti-Nephi-Lehies. They altered their entire way of life. They made a vow before God that they would never fight again. As an outward sign of this promise and of their faith, the men buried their swords in the ground.

The nearby Lamanites prepared to go to war against the Anti-Nephi-Lehies in battle. The righteous men still refused to fight and depended upon the Lord. The Lamanite armies descended upon the faithful and killed 1,005 unarmed men. "Now when the Lamanites saw that their brethren would not flee from the sword, neither would they turn aside to the right hand or to the left, but that they would lie down and perish, and praised God even in the very act of perishing under the sword—Now when the Lamanites saw this they did forbear from slaying them; and there were many whose hearts had swollen in them for those of their brethren who had fallen under the sword, for they repented of the things which they had done" (Alma 24:23–24). These men whose hearts were touched followed the example of the Anti-Nephi-Lehies and threw down their weapons. More than a thousand Lamanites repented and turned from wickedness.

The remaining Lamanites "swore vengeance upon the Nephites," but left the Anti-Nephi-Lehies alone for a time (Alma 25:1). There followed many battles between the Lamanites and the Nephites, with the Nephites emerging victorious. The Lamanites realized they were not going to defeat the Nephites, so they once again turned their attention to the Anti-Nephi-Lehies. The same terrible slaughter began against the people who were keeping their promise to the Lord to not fight.

Ammon could not stand by and watch his dear friends be killed. He went to the king and begged him to allow Ammon to lead the people to the Nephite land where they could be protected. The king was afraid the Nephites would have his people killed because of the terrible things they had done before they were converted. Ammon said that he would pray. The king assured Ammon that if the Lord directed him that they should go to the Nephite land, the king and his people would follow. Upon inquiring of the Lord, Ammon was told, "Get this people out of this land, that they perish not; for Satan has great hold on the hearts of the Amalekites, who do stir up the Lamanites to anger against their brethren to slay them; therefore get thee out of this land; and blessed are this people in this generation, for I will preserve them" (Alma 27:12). Relieved, Ammon, the king, and the Anti-Nephi-Lehies escaped to the land of Jershon where they were cared for and protected by the Nephites.

Many years passed and the Anti-Nephi-Lehies flourished under the watchful eye of the Nephites. Battles between the Lamanites and the Nephites continued to break out. Because of iniquities among the Nephite people, the Lamanites began to conquer. The Anti-Nephi-Lehies were distressed at the danger they felt they were bringing upon the Nephites in protecting them. "But it came to pass that when they saw the danger, and the many afflictions and tribulations which the Nephites bore for them, they were moved with compassion and were desirous to take up arms in the defence of their country" (Alma 53:13).

Ammon's friend Alma was a prophet. He had a son named Helaman who was a great military leader for the Nephites. Helaman was concerned that the Anti-Nephi-Lehies were considering breaking their oath with the Lord in order to help ward off the Lamanite attacks. Helaman was afraid for their souls if they should make such a choice; therefore he told them not to break their promise. These faithful men had to continue to watch their beloved protectors fall at the hands of the wicked Lamanites.

As the Anti-Nephi-Lehies mourned for their friends, a plan was being formed.

> But behold, it came to pass they had many sons, who had not entered into a covenant that they would not take their weapons of war to defend themselves against their enemies; therefore they did assemble themselves together at this time, as many as were able to take up arms, and they called themselves Nephites.
>
> And they entered into a covenant to fight for the liberty of the Nephites, yea, to protect the land unto the laying down of their lives; yea, even they covenanted that they never would give up their liberty, but they would fight in all cases to protect the Nephites and themselves from bondage.
>
> Now behold, there were two thousand of those young men, who entered into this covenant and took their weapons of war to defend their country. (Alma 53:16–18)

These young men are described as "exceedingly valiant for courage, and also for strength and activity; but behold, this was not all—they were men who were true at all times in whatsoever thing they were entrusted" (Alma 53:20). They were dependable. They chose Helaman to be their leader and marched into battle to assist their people.

Helaman sent a letter to Moroni after the fighting that described the events. He told Moroni that he went with his two thousand sons into battle. Helaman said he called them this because he loved them as sons and could depend on them. When they had arrived at Judea to help another military leader named Antipus, they discovered that most of the soldiers had been killed or taken prisoner. Antipus and his army were fighting desperately, but their morale was low. They were excited to see Helaman arrive with the two thousand stripling warriors. When the Lamanites saw the Nephites had been strengthened, they retreated somewhat. Helaman told Moroni that they did not want to go into the Lamanite strongholds for an attack, but wanted to try and coax the Lamanites out into their region. The fathers of the two thousand young men sent provisions for the soldiers, and another two thousand men arrived from the neighboring city of Zarahemla to help fight. Antipus devised a strategy for a surprise attack upon the Lamanites.

After fierce battles, the Nephites defeated the Lamanites. Helaman gave credit for the defeat to his two thousand dependable sons. He ordered that all his wounded young men should be brought off the battlefield away from the dead and have their wounds attended. Many Nephite soldiers died, but,

> There were two hundred, out of my two thousand and sixty, who had fainted because of the loss of blood; nevertheless, according to the goodness of God, and to our great astonishment, and also the joy of our whole army, there was not one soul of them who did perish; yea, and neither was there one soul among them who had not received many wounds.
>
> And now, their preservation was astonishing to our whole army, yea, that they should be spared while there was a thousand of our brethren who were slain. And we do justly ascribe it to the miraculous power of God, because of their exceeding faith in that which they had been taught to believe—that there was a just God, and whosoever did not doubt, that they should be preserved by his marvelous power.
>
> Now this was the faith of these of whom I have spoken; they are young, and their minds are firm, and they do put their trust in God continually. (Alma 57:25–27)

In a time of great turmoil and afflictions, two thousand young men rose to the challenge of defending all that was dear to them. Helaman learned these young men were dependable and had great faith, courage, and loyalty. Their people were counting on them to fight a battle only they could fight. They proved themselves to be men of strength and bravery, but most important, men of God.

Journal Prompt: Being dependable means people can count on you. What are some of the things your family depends upon you for? How can you be more dependable in some of your responsibilities?

Activity: Review or assign household chores or yard work. Make a point to be more dependable this week. Report next week how well you did in family home evening.

32. Modesty

Definition: Humble; having or showing a moderate estimation of one's own talents, abilities, and value; observing conventional proprieties in speech, behavior, or dress; quiet and humble in appearance; unpretentious.

Song: "Dearest Children, God Is Near You" (*Hymns*, 96)

Scriptures: Psalm 37:3–5; Alma 26:10–12; Helaman 12:5; D&C 41:1; D&C 76:5

The Beatitudes
Matthew 5:3–11

Modesty is often confused with how to dress. But modesty is more a state of mind. When we keep our hearts, minds, and spirits pure and modest, our dress will reflect that. One of the best lessons in modest living is found in the Sermon on the Mount when our Savior gave us the Beatitudes. The word *beatitude* is defined as "to be fortunate," "to be happy," or "to be blessed" (Matthew 5:3, footnote a). We will be fortunate, happy, and blessed when we do as the Lord teaches.

Let's go through the beatitudes one verse at a time to determine what modest and pure living is all about.

Matthew 5:3 says, "Blessed are the poor in spirit; for theirs is the kingdom of heaven." Poor in spirit does not mean being sad and depressed. It means having a contrite heart. We should not be proud, but humble. We should be humble in the way that we think of and present ourselves to God and people around us.

Verse four says, "Blessed are they that mourn: for they shall be comforted." When we grieve over something, the Lord is there to comfort us. Perhaps this seems to have little to do with modest living, but imagine someone who is sad but knows relief comes from the Lord. That person looks serene. He is at peace, not contentious or annoyed. This is the kind of person people want to be around, and be like.

Verse five says, "Blessed are the meek: for they shall inherit the earth." Meek people are humble, peaceful, and modest. Jesus gave attention to these specific characteristics, showing their importance. If we make a habit of being meek and humble, we are living more Christlike.

Verse six says, "Blessed are they which do hunger and thirst after righteousness: for they shall be filled." To hunger and thirst after something implies a longing for it. Instead of reading our scriptures, it might mean studying and searching and praying about them. Instead of saying a simple, routine prayer, it might mean pouring out our hearts to our Heavenly Father and spending more time talking to Him. Instead of making sure our daily activities get done, it might mean seeking out those who need our help and trying to make a difference in our communities. Articles of Faith 1:13 gives us the standard for the righteous things for which we should hunger and thirst: "If there is anything virtuous, lovely, or of good report or praiseworthy, we seek after these things."

Verse seven says, "Blessed are the merciful: for they shall obtain mercy." Mercy is the kind and compassionate treatment of a person. A Primary song says, "Jesus said love everyone; Treat them kindly, too. When your heart is filled with love, Others will love you ("Jesus Said Love Everyone," *Children's Songbook,* 61). The lesson is simple. Jesus wants us to extend mercy. In return, we receive that same mercy.

Verse eight says, "Blessed are the pure in heart: for they shall see God." Keeping our hearts pure is a tough thing in the world today. We are continually assaulted with foul language, pornography, and violence. Heavenly Father has blessed us with discernment and the ability to receive personal revelation. We must be modest in what we choose to watch and listen to. If we are unsure of the merit of some television show, movie, music, or reading material, we should determine if the Spirit can be present in such an atmosphere. Keeping our hearts pure is important, for those who do shall see God.

Verse nine says, "Blessed are the peacemakers: for they shall be called the children of God." Being a peacemaker is often difficult, especially if you have brothers and sisters. Heavenly Father knows this can be a struggle and is there to help you when you pray to Him. Being a peacemaker in terms of modesty may mean not arguing to win a fight or not boasting of an accomplishment to make someone jealous. A home free from contention is vital if we are going to combat the influences of the world. If you look for the bad in everyone and everything around you, that is what you will find. Fortunately, the same holds true when you look for the good, which is what we should do to find and keep peace in our homes.

Verse ten says, "Blessed are they which are persecuted for righteousness' sake: for theirs is the kingdom of heaven." There are always going to be those who do not understand what we believe, or who choose not to. We still have an obligation to treat those people with kindness and be modest. However, we are under no obligation to hide our faith. In fact, we must carry our faith like a flag for all to see. That may mean that someone will laugh at us, tease us, or say unkind things to us. While it may not be easy, Heavenly Father will help us to bear whatever we suffer in His name, just as He helped the early Saints.

The Beatitudes are a reminder of how to live a modest life. When we follow our Savior's teachings in His Sermon on the Mount, we live the way He intends us to, not the way the world would have us live. This is what is meant by being in the world and not of the world.

Journal Prompt: Have you had an experience where you were uncomfortable in some clothing or with some form of media you saw? Write about the value of having promptings from the Spirit in these situations.

Activity: Have a Modesty Fashion Show with your family. Play appropriate music. Talk about what styles of clothing and what forms of media are appropriate.

33. Helpfulness

Definition: Providing help; useful.

Song: "You Can Make the Pathway Bright" (*Hymns,* 228)

Scriptures: 1 Peter 3:8–12; Mosiah 2:17, 41

Samuel the Lamanite
Helaman 13–16

There was a Lamanite man named Samuel who believed in the Lord and wanted to teach others about the gospel. He went about preaching to an increasingly wicked population of Nephites. He warned them of the dangers of living in sin and urged them to repent. Samuel went to the Nephite city of Zarahemla about six years before Christ was born. He preached to the people for several days about the approaching birth of the Savior, but they threw him out of the city. Samuel was planning to return to his home when the Lord spoke to Samuel, telling him to return to the city and speak whatever came into his heart.

Samuel did as he had been commanded, but the people would not let him enter. Samuel's desire to help these people escape their destruction and his obedience to God spurred him on. Instead of retreating, Samuel climbed up on the wall that surrounded the city of Zarahemla, raised his hands, and began to cry out to the people. He told the people that he was speaking the words the Lord had put in his mouth. He called out, saying within four hundred years, they would all be destroyed if they did not turn from their wicked ways. He had come to announce the glorious birth of the Savior, but because he had not been received, he was there to warn them of their destruction. Samuel told them the Lord would not allow them to continue in unrighteousness. The Lord would destroy them if they continued to harden their hearts against Him. The only reason their destruction had not already come upon them was that there still remained a few righteous individuals in the city. Samuel prophesied the wicked would soon get rid of any righteous people, and then the city would be "ripe for destruction" (Helaman 13:14).

Samuel also warned the people about their love of material things. They had been focusing their attention on earthly treasures instead of on the Lord. Samuel said, "Ye do not remember the Lord your God in the things with which he hath blessed you, but ye do always remember your riches, not to thank the Lord your God for them; yea, your hearts are not drawn out unto the Lord, but they do swell with great pride, unto boasting" (Helaman 13:22). Their desires for material possessions over their love of God would end in a curse on their heads.

Samuel discouraged the people from ignoring and mistreating prophets who tried to help people find the joy of the gospel. The day was swiftly coming when they would wish they had repented of their sins. They were living on borrowed time, and that *now* was the time to act.

Samuel now told them about the birth of the Savior. He prophesied to the people of a great sign that would accompany Jesus' birth. Many people would fall to the earth crying repentance and believing in Christ when they saw those signs. Those who believe would have everlasting life.

Samuel explained Christ was coming to atone for our sins. Jesus would be resurrected so that we could all be resurrected and return to live with our Heavenly Father again. The people who did not repent would suffer a second death—a spiritual death, which would cut them off from the presence of the Lord forever. This is why, Samuel explained, he had come to talk with them.

Samuel told the people of another sign—the sign for the death of the Savior. He said, "The sun shall be darkened and refuse to give his light . . . there shall be no light upon the face of this land . . . for the space of three days, to the time that he shall rise again from the dead" (Helaman 14:20).

Samuel also told the Nephites a very important thing concerning agency. He said, "And now remember, remember, my brethren, that whosoever perisheth, perisheth unto himself; and whosoever doeth iniquity, doeth it unto himself; for behold, ye are free; ye are permitted to act for yourselves; for behold, God hath given unto you a knowledge and he hath made you free" (Helaman 14:30).

Many people who heard Samuel as he preached upon the wall did experience a change of heart. They went in search of Nephi the missionary and asked to be baptized.

There were those, however, who grew angry at Samuel's words. They threw stones and shot arrows at him, "but the Spirit of the Lord was with him, insomuch that they could not hit him with their stones neither with their arrows" (Helaman 16:2). The fact that Samuel could not be harmed startled the people. Some of them even went to Nephi to be baptized because they knew that Samuel was being protected by God. The most hardened still refused to believe and grew even angrier. They called guards to bind Samuel and take him away. They accused Samuel of being possessed by a devil. These people were so deeply entrenched in their sinful lives that they refused to recognize a prophet of God as he stood on a wall before them.

Samuel escaped before the guards reached him. He returned to his own land and continued preaching the gospel. The Nephites of Zarahemla never saw him again.

Samuel the Lamanite loved his brethren so much that he placed himself in a life-threatening position on their behalf. He did not teach only his friends and neighbors. Samuel went where the Lord sent him. He preached to people who sought to take away his life. He boldly shared the gospel and urged repentance to the masses who wanted no part of him or his message. Samuel referred to these people who reviled him as "my beloved brethren" (Helaman 15:1). He wanted nothing more than to help the Nephites who had gone astray. He wanted to show them the way back to Heavenly Father. We can give this same kind of help when we share the gospel today.

Journal Prompt: Samuel helped his brethren by spreading the gospel. How can you help your neighbors? What are some of the ways you can share the gospel with your "brethren"?

Activity: Gather any clothing, toys, or household items you no longer use and donate them to a local shelter or charitable group. Talk about your blessings and how by donating these things you are sharing those blessings with others.

34. Steadfastness

Definition: Fixed or unchanging; steady; firmly loyal or constant.

Song: "How Firm a Foundation" (*Hymns,* 85)

Scriptures: Isaiah 41:10, 43:2–5; Helaman 5:12, 15:10

Job's Strength of Conviction
Job 1–2, 23

Job was a man of God; the Lord describes Job as "a perfect and an upright man, one that feareth God, and escheweth evil" (Job 2:3). He had seven sons, three daughters, many animals, and "a very great household; so that this man was the greatest of all the men of the east" (Job 1:3). Job was well known in his part of the world. He had all the material possessions he could want, but he loved the Lord more than all his things. He was compassionate to the less fortunate and had many friends. He praised Heavenly Father and gave thanks for all the blessings he had been given.

Satan was aware of Job and his love of God. He told God that Job was only good and kind because he had been so blessed in his life and challenged God to test Job's faith. Satan said, "But put forth thine hand now, and touch all that he hath, and he will curse thee to thy face" (Job 1:11). The Lord allowed Satan to test Job's faith.

One day Job's servant came to tell him that an Arab tribe called the Sabeans had attacked Job's servants in the field, killing them all and stealing the oxen and donkeys. Only this one messenger had survived.

While this servant spoke, another messenger arrived. He related a tragic story saying, "The fire of God is fallen from heaven, and hath burned up the sheep, and the servants, and consumed them; and I only am escaped alone to tell thee" (Job 1:16).

During this conversation, another of Job's servants came to relay the circumstances of yet another calamity. This messenger informed Job that the Chaldeans of Babylon had killed the servants who were with Job's camels and then stole the camels. Job's servant who delivered the news was the sole survivor.

Job was then approached by a fourth servant, who brought news far worse than any thus far. This man told Job, "Thy sons and thy daughters were eating and drinking wine in their eldest brother's house: And behold there came a great wind from the wilderness, and smote the four corners of the house, and it fell upon the young men, and they are dead; and I only am escaped alone to tell thee" (Job 1:18–19).

Job was distraught. He tore his clothing and shaved his head, as was the custom for great mourning. Satan said Job would no longer worship God if Job had to endure personal bodily afflictions. Satan said, "All that man hath will he give for his life. But put forth thine hand now, and touch his bone and his flesh, and he will curse thee to thy face" (Job 2:4–5). Satan was once again allowed to tempt Job, but the Lord warned Satan, "Behold, he is in thine hand; but save his life" (v. 6). Job was stricken with sores on his body from head to toe. These sores were hideous to look at; they oozed and were itchy. After all this devastation, Job's wife even asked him, "Dost thou still retain thine integrity? curse God, and die" (v. 9). Job asked his wife if they should accept good from God and not accept the bad. "In all this did Job not sin with his lips" (Job 2:10).

Three of Job's friends heard of what had befallen him and they came to see Job. His friends were Eliphaz, Bildad, and Zophar. They had planned to join together to comfort Job. The change in Job was so great that his friends didn't even recognize him when they arrived. They were saddened by his condition and sat with him for seven days and nights before even speaking. Job began to cry to his friends in anguish. He said that he wished he had never even been born.

At this point, Job's friends began, in turn, to criticize Job. They reprimanded him for resisting what they saw as justified punishment from God for some transgression in Job's life. They told Job that God would never allow such terrible things to come upon someone unless they had sinned terribly. Job insisted that he was free from any such sin, and that he loved the Lord. His friends said this was not possible; obviously Job was being punished, and he should welcome this correction from God. They further stated that if he turned away from his sin, God would remove these curses from Job's life.

Job told his friends the afflicted should be comforted and supported, not condemned. Job asked God and his friends what he had done that was sinful. His friends continued to accuse and belittle him.

The men persisted in their persecution of Job, but Job remained steadfast in the knowledge of his virtue. He called upon the Lord saying, "Oh that I knew where I might find him! that I might come even to his seat! I would order my cause before him, and fill my mouth with arguments. I would know the words which he would answer me, and understand what he would say unto me. Will he plead against me with his great power? No; but he would put his strength in me: . . . Behold I go forward but he is not there; . . . But he knoweth the way that I take: when he hath tried me, I shall come forth as gold" (Job 23:3–10). Even though Job remained in a state of misery, he recognized that through our adversities, the Lord is able to turn us into something beautiful, like gold.

After many more interchanges with these men who plagued Job, the Lord spoke. He told Job of His great power and reprimanded the friends. Job repented of his complaints and acknowledged God's hand in all things. Job was given twice as much as he had formerly had. He lived another one hundred and forty years, being able to enjoy many generations of his family.

In the face of trials people often wonder, "Why me?" We have been given the book of Job, which clearly illustrates the fact that good people suffer. Our afflictions may sometimes be brought upon us by own actions, but sometimes bad things just happen to good people. Perhaps we are being tested or perhaps we are being made into the gold of which Job spoke. At any rate, our response to these trials is the thing that is most telling. Are we the kind of people who return adversity with complaint or will we stand steadfast in times of adversity?

Journal Prompt: During all his trials, Job tried to remain steadfast. What things in your life will help you strengthen your faith to withstand trials?

Activity: Create a rope course or an obstacle course in the dark to practice staying on track. Celebrate "staying the course" with a special treat.

35. Enthusiasm

Definition: Strong or intense feeling; eagerness; zeal.

Song: "We Are All Enlisted" (*Hymns*, 250)

Scriptures: Psalm 40:8; D&C 19:29, 37–39

A Candle under a Bushel
Luke 11:33–36

Soon after calling His twelve apostles, Jesus counseled them as they began their missionary work. This counsel is referred to as the Sermon on the Mount. The Savior gave a similar sermon to His apostles in the Americas.

One of the lessons Jesus gave was of enthusiasm for the gospel. He demonstrated this teaching, as He often did, in a parable. He said, "No man, when he hath lighted a candle, putteth it in a secret place, neither under a bushel, but on a candlestick, that they which come in may see the light" (Luke 11:33). Our candle is the light of Christ. It is our knowledge of and love for our Savior that fills us with light. The Apostle Paul wrote, "For ye were sometimes darkness, but now are ye light in the Lord: walk as children of light" (Ephesians 5:8). When we share the gospel with others, we are walking as "children of light." We have been given the wonderful gift of having the restored gospel, but not everyone is as fortunate as we are. This is why missionary work is so important. There are people throughout the world who, even as we speak, are waiting and searching for the light that we have. The full-time missionaries are not the only ones who can bring truth to them. It is our duty to find those people and share our light.

We can let our candle shine in many ways. Jesus said, "Let your light so shine before men, that they may see your good works, and glorify your Father which is in heaven" (Matthew 5:16). One of the best ways to share our light is by setting a good example. Our actions are observed by people more than we know. Our behavior indicates what we believe, for as the Savior said, "No man can serve two masters" (Matthew 6:24). When people see us following the teachings of Jesus, they see our light.

Another way our light shines is in our countenance. When we appear down and depressed, nobody wants to be like us. When we show the happiness that comes from following our Savior, however, people want to experience that joy for themselves. Try the smiling game—smile at everyone you see. Most people can't help but smile back. It's contagious! People pay special attention when we have the light of Christ, which is "enlightenment, knowledge, and an uplifting, ennobling, persevering influence that comes upon mankind because of Jesus Christ" (Bible Dictionary, "Light of Christ," 725). In essence, we want to do better and be better because of the gospel. Sometimes seeing that "special something" in us that people can't quite define is all it takes to open the door for a person to receive the gospel.

The Savior warns us against hiding our candle under a bushel (or basket) or in a secret place. A candle's purpose is to shine. We wouldn't be embarrassed to light a candle in a dark room, and we need not be shy about helping to light our little part of a dark world with the light of Christ. Whether it is in our actions or our countenance, our light will shine forth when we hold up our candles with enthusiasm.

Journal Prompt: What can you do to be a better member missionary? After the activity, record your experiences.

Activity: As a family, pray about a date on which the missionaries can come into your home to teach a nonmember friend, family member, or neighbor the gospel. Write the date and post it somewhere in your home. Contact the person and the missionaries in your area and prepare your home for a teaching environment. Prepare to see great things happen!

36. Obedience

Definition: Carrying out a request or command; dutiful.

Song: "I Will Follow God's Plan" (*Children's Songbook,* 164)

Scriptures: Mosiah 2:41; Abraham 3:25–26

Joshua and the Battle of Jericho
Joshua 1–6

The Lord's people whom He had brought out of captivity were mourning the death of their leader, Moses. God had called a new leader, Joshua. The Israelites had been wandering in the wilderness and were now at the River Jordan (see Bible Map 10: Canaan in Old Testament Times). The Lord told Joshua that the people would soon cross the river and would overtake the city Jericho. He said, "Every place that the sole of your foot shall tread upon, that have I given unto you, as I said unto Moses. . . . There shall not any man be able to stand before thee all the days of thy life: as I was with Moses, so I will be with thee: I will not fail thee, nor forsake thee. Be strong and of good courage: for unto this people shalt thou divide for an inheritance the land, which I sware unto their fathers to give them" (Joshua 1:3–6). Joshua told the people about the Lord's plan for them to cross the Jordan, and they supported him.

Jericho was a walled city. Joshua sent two spies into Jericho. The two men were taken in by a woman named Rahab. Word got out that Israelite spies had infiltrated the city, so some of the men of Jericho searched for them. They came to Rahab's home and asked her if she had seen the spies.

She told them she had seen the men running away toward another part of the city. But really, she had hidden the Israelites on her rooftop.

Rahab told the spies the whole city feared their people because they heard how Moses crossed the Red Sea on dry ground. She knew the God of Israel could save her and beseeched the spies to spare her and her family when they took Jericho. In return for the kindness Rahab had shown them, Joshua's men promised that neither she nor her family would be injured. They instructed her to hang a red "thread" from her window to alert the soldiers, who were told not to harm that particular household (Joshua 2:18). Rahab did as they instructed and was, with her family, the sole survivor of the destruction that came upon Jericho.

Even though Rahab believed that the God of Israel could protect her, many people in the city of Jericho felt safe from attack. Jericho had a tall wall all the way around it. Joshua, however, had the Lord on his side. Joshua received very specific instructions from God on how to proceed. The Jordan River was between the Israelites and Jericho. Joshua was told to have priests carry the ark of the covenant into the Jordan River. When they did so, the waters of the river "which came down from above stood and rose up upon an heap" (Joshua 3:16). The Israelites were once again able to cross on dry land a place that is usually flooded with water. The Lord spoke to Joshua and told him to get twelve men, one of every tribe, and have them each take a rock from the middle of the Jordan River. As soon as they carried the ark of the covenant up the bank of the river, the Lord caused the river to resume its flow. Joshua placed the twelve rocks in Gilgal, where they stopped. He explained that the rocks were to serve as a reminder of all the Lord had done for them.

Joshua's next task was to take the city of Jericho. God once again told Joshua what to do. Seven priests were called to carry rams' horns. These men blew the horns and began to walk around the walled city of Jericho, followed by the armed Israelites, the ark of the covenant, and the rest of the people. Joshua instructed the people to remain silent until he told them to shout. The group made their way around Jericho one time and went back to camp in silence. They did this same thing, according to the Lord's command, for six days. On the seventh day, they went through the same motions; except that they circled the city seven times. The priests blew their horns and Joshua cried out, "Shout; for the Lord hath given you the city" (Joshua 6:16). When the people shouted, the walls of Jericho fell to the ground.

Joshua told the Israelites to take the city but to keep Rahab and her family safe. The two spies Joshua had originally sent into Jericho brought Rahab and her family out, but the rest of the city was completely destroyed.

Joshua was obedient to all the Lord required of him. He was called to lead his people, to cross a river that was made dry land; and to capture and destroy a seemingly impenetrable city. Each of these tasks appeared to be impossible. Joshua knew, though, that through obedience to the will of the Lord, all things are possible.

Journal Prompt: Obedience is a very important virtue to develop because there is safety in obeying commandments and laws. How does obeying Heavenly Father's commandments keep you safe? How does obeying your parents' rules keep you safe? How does obeying the laws of your land keep you safe?

Activity: Act out the story of Joshua and the battle of Jericho. Make rams' horns by rolling paper into a cone and taping it. Use bathrobes, nightgowns, or sheets as costumes. Build your own walled city using your furniture and household objects (the back of the couch makes a nice wall, but it doesn't fall as nicely as a stack of toys does!). Blue fabric (sheets, blankets, or towels) on the floor might be the River Jordan. Get creative and have fun!

37. Prayerfulness

Definition: Inclined to pray frequently.

Song: "Did You Think to Pray?" (*Hymns,* 140)

Scriptures: Psalm 104:34; Alma 34:18–27, Alma 37:37

Prayer of Enos
Enos 1

As Nephi grew old, he passed the record of his family on the brass plates to his brother Jacob. When he, too, became an old man, Jacob gave the plates to his son, Enos. The book of Enos is only one chapter, but it tells a wonderful story.

Enos tells of his "wrestle" before God when he was praying for a remission of his sins (Enos 1:2). He had gone hunting one day and was thinking about some things his father had taught him. He said, "And the words which I had often heard my father speak concerning eternal life, and the joy of the saints, sunk deep into my heart" (v. 3). Enos says that his soul hungered. He had a great desire to develop his own testimony of the Lord and to repent of his sins. Enos knelt in the forest and cried to God in prayer. He prayed all day and "when the night came I did still raise my voice high that it reached the heavens" (v. 4).

After some time, the Lord spoke to Enos, saying, "Enos, thy sins are forgiven thee, and thou shalt be blessed" (Enos 1:5). Enos said he knew that the Lord could not lie, so he no longer felt guilty about his past sins.

After hearing these things from the Lord, Enos says he "began to feel a desire for the welfare of my brethren, the Nephites; wherefore, I did pour out my whole soul unto God for them" (Enos 1:9). Enos was satisfied that his sins had been forgiven, and he wanted his people to have the same assurance. The Lord again spoke to Enos, telling him that God would bless the Nephites. He told Enos He had given the Nephite people a holy land; and as long as they obeyed His commandments they would prosper. Enos said that "after I, Enos, had heard these words, my faith began to be unshaken in the Lord" (v. 11).

Enos then began to pray fervently for the Lamanites. He prayed that if the Nephites were destroyed and the Lamanites survived, the Lord would preserve the plates for a time when the Lamanites would be willing to hear the gospel. The Lamanites had hardened their hearts against the Lord and promised to destroy the plates if they could. He prayed until the Lord said to him, "Whatsoever thing ye shall ask in faith, believing that ye shall receive in the name of Christ, ye shall receive it" (Enos 1:15). Enos had great faith; therefore, the Lord promised him that the records would be preserved.

The prayers of Enos continued from morning until night. Enos sought the Lord's help for his own salvation, for his people, and for his enemies. He poured out his soul to the Lord and was given peace and direction. We have been instructed to do as Enos did. Heavenly Father wants to hear the prayers of our hearts.

Journal Prompt: Write about a time that you received an answer to prayer. Not all prayers are answered in the way that we want, but Heavenly Father always hears us when we pray. Why do you think He wants so much to hear from you?

Activity: Talk about the specific needs and blessings of family members. Write down those needs and blessings. Post the paper on the refrigerator or some other place where all can see it. Pray specifically for each other.

38. Peacefulness

Definition: Undisturbed by strife, turmoil, or disagreement; tranquil.

Song: "Master, the Tempest Is Raging" (*Hymns,* 105)

Scriptures: 1 Samuel 20:42; Matthew 8:23–27; Mosiah 15:14–18; D&C 105:38–40

"Peace, Be Still"
Mark 4:35–41

Jesus and His twelve apostles were in Capernaum near the Sea of Galilee (see Bible Map 11: The Holy Land in New Testament Times). He was on the shore, but so many people gathered to hear Him that Jesus decided to board a ship so the crowds could better see and hear. Jesus taught the people in four parables. After the crowd dispersed, Jesus was left alone with His apostles. The twelve talked with Jesus for some time about the parables He had shared that day. Jesus then retired to the back of the ship to rest.

While He was sleeping, a storm arose on the Sea of Galilee. The Bible Dictionary tells us that at the Sea of Galilee "the heat is very great, and the cold air rushing down from the hills often produces sudden storms" ("Galilee, Sea of," 677). The storm raged and Mark said, "The waves beat into the ship, so that it was now full" (Mark 4:37). This was frightening for the twelve men. Their ship was being tossed about, winds were howling, waves were washing onto the ship, and they were taking on water.

The apostles rushed into the part of the ship where the Savior was. To their astonishment, Jesus lay on a pillow, fast asleep. They awakened Jesus and related their plight, crying, "Master, carest thou not that we perish?" (Mark 4:38).

Jesus calmly arose and "rebuked the wind, and said unto the sea, Peace, be still" (Mark 4:39). The storm ceased immediately. Everything was calm and peaceful. Jesus turned to His apostles and said, "Why are ye so fearful? how is it that ye have no faith?" (v. 40).

This is a story of peace. Jesus said, "Peace, be still," and all was calm. He says the same to us today. This world in which we live is much like a tempest-tossed sea. There are real dangers facing us, just as the waves threatened the apostles' ship. The message of our Savior is to have faith in Him and to quiet our spirits that we may hear the promptings of the Holy Ghost. Just as Jesus calmed the sea, He can bring peace into our lives. We have no need to fear; we need only have faith in Him.

Journal Prompt: Name some times when you have felt peace. Name some places where you have felt peace. How can you have those feelings more often in your life?

Activity: Make small boats from household supplies. You can use disposable foil mini loaf pans, playdough, empty walnut shells, and so forth for the vessel. Use toothpicks and small bits of construction paper to make a mast and sails. Glue the mast and sails onto the boat. Sail the boats in the bathtub, sink, a ditch, or other pool of water. Create a tempest and then calm the waters. Talk about the different effects chaos and peace can have in our lives.

39. Gratitude

Definition: The state of being grateful to a benefactor; thankfulness

Song: "Because I Have Been Given Much" (*Hymns,* 219)

Scriptures: Psalm 36:7, Psalm 68:19; Jacob 2:17–19

Hannah's Song
1 Samuel 1–2

*I*n Old Testament times, it was customary for a man to have more than one wife. A man named Elkanah lived in a place called Ephraim (see Bible Map 3: The Division of the 12 Tribes) with his family and had two wives—Hannah and Peninnah. Elkanah and Peninnah had children together, but Hannah was barren, meaning she was unable to bear children. This was very troubling to Hannah, who desperately wanted to have a child with her husband. To make matters worse, Peninnah was unkind to Hannah about her situation. In fact, Peninnah provoked her so much that Hannah cried and cried. Hannah couldn't even eat, she was so sad. All she wanted was to have a baby. Elkanah tried to console his wife. He said, "Hannah, why weepest thou? and why eatest thou not? and why is thy heart grieved? am not I better to thee than ten sons?" (1 Samuel 1:8). But Hannah remained inconsolable.

Every year Elkanah took his family and traveled to the tabernacle in Shiloh to worship. This tabernacle is the same temple the Israelites had in the wilderness that housed the ark of the covenant. On this trip to the tabernacle, Hannah went in to pray. Hannah's heart was heavy and she cried as she prayed to the Lord for help. She promised the Lord that if He would bless her with a son, she would bring the child to the tabernacle and "give him unto the Lord all the days of his life" (1 Samuel 1:11). Hannah uttered this prayer silently in her heart, but she moved her lips as she prayed. The priest, Eli, saw her and asked what she had been doing. When Hannah told Eli that she had been praying, he said to her, "Go in peace: and the God of Israel grant thee thy petition that thou hast asked of him" (v. 17).

Hannah left, and "her countenance was no more sad" (1 Samuel 1:18). Hannah had great faith. She no longer troubled over the matter and the Lord blessed her with a son. If this was the end of the story, it would teach us a great lesson in faith. We are, however, going to see gratitude as we read the rest of the story.

Hannah and Elkanah named their little boy Samuel, which means "name of God" (Bible Dictionary, "Samuel," 768). Hannah said she chose this name "Because I have asked him of the Lord" (1 Samuel 1:20). When it came time to take their annual trip to Shiloh to the tabernacle, Hannah stayed home with baby Samuel because he was still nursing. When he had been weaned, though, Hannah brought her young son to the tabernacle. She found Eli and said, "O my lord, as thy soul liveth, my lord, I am the woman that stood by thee here, praying unto the Lord. For this child I prayed; and the Lord hath given me my petition which I asked of him: Therefore also I have lent him to the Lord; as long as he liveth he shall be lent to the Lord" (vv. 26–28).

After Hannah delivered her young son to Eli, she prayed a prayer which has been called Hannah's Song.

Hannah's Song

My heart rejoiceth in the Lord, mine horn is exalted in the Lord: my mouth is enlarged over mine enemies; because I rejoice in thy salvation.

There is none holy as the Lord: for there is none beside thee: neither is there any rock like our God.

Talk no more so exceeding proudly; let not arrogancy come out of your mouth: for the Lord is a God of knowledge, and by him actions are weighed.

The bows of the mighty men are broken, and they that stumbled are girded with strength.

They that were full have hired out themselves for bread; and they that were hungry ceased: so that the barren hath born seven; and she that hath many children is waxed feeble.

The Lord killeth, and maketh alive: he bringeth down to the grave, and bringeth up.

The Lord maketh poor, and maketh rich: he bringeth low, and lifteth up.

He raiseth up the poor out of the dust, and lifteth up the beggar from the dunghill, to set them among princes, and to make them inherit the throne of glory: for the pillars of the earth are the Lord's, and he hath set the world upon them.

He will keep the feet of his saints, and the wicked shall be silent in darkness; for by strength shall no man prevail.

The adversaries of the Lord shall be broken to pieces; out of heaven shall he thunder upon them: the Lord shall judge the ends of the earth; and he shall give strength unto his king, and exalt the horn of his anointed. (1 Samuel 2:1–10).

Samuel remained in the tabernacle. He served the Lord his whole life. Hannah's song of praise is humbling. She is truly an example to all of how to show gratitude to the Lord.

Journal Prompt: What are some of the gifts with which the Lord has blessed you? How can you show your gratitude to Him in return?

Activity: Make an "I Am Grateful" mobile. Write down the things you are grateful for on brightly colored paper. Attach string to each paper and tie the other end of the string to a coat hanger, dowel, or stick. Hang the mobile in your home.

40. Boldness

Definition: Fearless and daring; courageous.

Song: "Choose the Right" (*Hymns,* 239)

Scriptures: Proverbs 28:1; John 7:26; Alma 18:24

Gideon Leads an Army
Judges 6–8

After the death of the Israelites leader Joshua, the Lord gave the people judges to guide them instead of a king. The Judges is a "period of history between Joshua and Saul, extending over some 200 years, and marked by disorder, idolatry, and foreign oppression. The judge was more than a civil officer. He was generally a military leader as well, and his right to lead rested on the fact that in the eyes of the people he was the strongest and best man for the purpose. Faith in God was always the secret to success; but as a rule the judge was more of a fighter than a preacher" (Bible Dictionary, "The Judges," 719). During this time, the Israelites became divided. They were still united in worshipping the same God, but there began to be tensions among different groups.

As the Israelites' faith decreased, the Lord allowed them to come into bondage to various surrounding kingdoms. At the time of our story of Gideon, the people had been in bondage to the Midianites (see Bible Map 9: The World of the Old Testament) for seven years. The Israelites suffered greatly at the hand of these people. Every time the Israelites began to prosper in the land, the Midianites would steal their animals and destroy their crops. The people cried unto the Lord for rescue. In response to their prayers, the Lord sent a prophet to the people to remind them of the miracles that had been performed in their behalf and to instruct them on their responsibility to obey the commandments.

At this time a man named Gideon was called by God to break the Midianite control over the Lord's people. The Lord came to Gideon and told him that he was the one chosen to free the people. Gideon responded in a way that I think most of us would have: "Oh my Lord, wherewith shall I save Israel? Behold, my family is poor in Manasseh, and I am the least in my father's house" (Judges 6:15). Gideon was afraid and unsure of himself, and yet he was willing to do the will of God. The Lord said, "Surely I will be with thee, and thou shalt smite the Midianites as one man" (v. 16). This must have been an amazing thing to Gideon, but he obeyed the Lord's instructions.

Gideon gathered an army together and prepared to face the Midianites. But the Lord told Gideon that he had too many men in his army! He said, "The people that are with thee are too many for me to give the Midianites into their hands, lest Israel vaunt themselves against me, saying, Mine own hand hath saved me" (Judge 7:2). The Israelites were still so proud that if this huge army had overtaken their enemies, they would have taken the credit for themselves. He told Gideon to tell his soldiers that any of them who were afraid could turn and go back home. Twenty-two thousand men left; ten thousand remained. Still, the Lord said this army was too large. He told Gideon to bring the troops to the river for water. The men who bent down on their knees to drink from the river and those who lapped the water with their tongues like dogs were sent away. Those who drank water they scooped up in their hands stayed as Gideon's army. Gideon ended up with three hundred men. "And the Lord said unto Gideon, By the three hundred men that lapped [putting their hand to their mouth] will I save you, and deliver the Midianites into thine hand" (v. 7).

That night the Lord told Gideon to go to the edge of the Midianite camp and listen. He said what Gideon would hear would strengthen him. Gideon and his servant Phurah did as they had been told. While there, they heard a man tell another of a dream he had had in which a cake of barley bread tumbled down into the Midianite camp and knocked over a tent, laying the tent flat. The other man said the dream meant "the sword of Gideon the son of Joash, a man of Israel: for unto his hand hath God delivered Midian, and all the host" (Judges 7:14). Gideon praised God and returned to the Israelite camp. He told his three hundred men to "arise; for the Lord hath delivered into your hand the host of Midian" (v. 15).

Gideon divided his three hundred soldiers into three groups of one hundred each. Each man was given a trumpet and a pitcher with a torch inside it. They surrounded the Midianite camp. Gideon instructed his men, saying, "When I blow with a trumpet, I and all that are with me, then blow ye the trumpets also on every side of all the camp, and say, The sword of the Lord, and of Gideon" (Judges 7:18).

Gideon took one group of a hundred men and they all proceeded to surround the camp. On Gideon's signal, all the men blew their trumpets, broke the pitchers, and cried out, "The sword of the Lord, and of Gideon" (Judges 7:20). The Midianites were so startled and confused that they cried out and fled.

Gideon sent troops out to defeat the Midianites. The Lord truly worked a miracle through the boldness of Gideon, who trusted in God.

Journal Prompt: Often we are given specific instructions from the Lord. What is the difference in following with fear or with boldness? Sometimes other people do not understand the choices we make in following the Lord. Write about an opportunity you had when you felt bold for following the commandments.

Activity: Act out the story of Gideon using paper bags as pitchers with flashlights underneath as the torches. Roll construction paper into cone shapes to be trumpets. Surround the Midianite camp, blow your trumpets, break your pitchers, and shout, "The sword of the Lord, and of Gideon!" Talk about how to be bold in following the instructions of the Lord. The corn chip snack Bugles makes a great treat with this lesson.

41. Reverence

Definition: Special esteem or respect.

Song: "Teach Me to Walk in the Light" (*Children's Songbook,* 177)

Scriptures about Reverence: Leviticus 19:30; Ecclesiastes 5:1; Hebrews 12:28; D&C 107:4

Jesus Cleanses the Temple
Mark 11:15–19

Jesus had recently begun teaching, preaching, and performing miracles in His ministry. He traveled to Jerusalem by donkey and, upon His arrival, was greeted by the people with shouts of "Hosanna!" Jesus went to the temple in Jerusalem and found there a disturbing sight. Inside the temple, people were buying and selling goods. Jesus was filled with righteous indignation, meaning He was justified in His anger. He turned over the tables that the merchants were using, disrupting their business.

The temple has always been a place for reverence. Jesus said, "Is it not written, My house shall be called of all nations the house of prayer? but ye have made it into a den of thieves" (Mark 11:17). He was disappointed in the lack of reverence in His house. Matthew tells us that after cleansing the temple, Jesus healed the blind and lame who came to Him. Can you see the two images of the temple? One is the market-type atmosphere with all its noise and busyness; the second is of the presence of His calm power as the Savior performed miracles.

Reverence is just as important today as it was on that day in the temple in Jerusalem. The temple is the Lord's house. We know to use hushed voices and to let the Spirit speak to us when on temple grounds. There are other sacred and reverent places too. Our church buildings, specifically the chapel, are also the Lord's house. This is why the Primary children sing, "Our chapel is a sacred place; We enter quietly. Dear Father, while we sing and pray, Our thoughts will be of thee" ("Our Chapel Is a Sacred Place," *Children's Songbook*, 30).

Another sacred, reverent place is our home. This is not to say that we should tiptoe and whisper through our house, but it should always be a place where the Spirit can abide. Our home should be a haven from the world, a place of peace and love. We strive to create an atmosphere free from contention where all who enter feel a special something that we know as the Spirit of the Lord.

Journal Prompt: How do you feel when you are in a reverent place such as the temple, the chapel as the sacrament is passed, or your home during family prayer? What can you do to help create a reverent atmosphere?

Activity: Visit a temple if there is one near you. Enjoy the beauty and reverence of the grounds. If you do not have a temple nearby, look at pictures of different temples around the world.

42. Calmness

Definition: Not excited or agitated; composed; serenity; tranquility; peace.

Song: "Jesus, the Very Thought of Thee" (*Hymns,* 141)

Scriptures: Psalm 104:34; Proverbs 1:33; Isaiah 32:17–18

David and Goliath
1 Samuel 17

When the Israelites were in Judah, the Philistines came to battle against them (see Bible Map 3: The Division of the 12 Tribes). The Israelites were on one mountain; the Philistines were on another, with a valley between them. The Philistine army unveiled their secret weapon— a giant over nine feet tall, named Goliath. Goliath challenged any of them that dared to come fight him. He said if an Israelite could defeat him, the Philistines would serve them. If, however, he was victorious, the Israelites would become slaves to the Philistines. The Israelites were terrified; no one would accept the challenge.

Many young men left their homes in Judah to follow King Saul into battle against the Philistines. Among these young men were three of the sons of Jesse of Bethlehem. Their younger brother, David, had stayed home with their father to tend the family's sheep. Jesse asked David to take food to his brothers and to find out how they were.

When he arrived at the Israelite camp, David heard about Goliath's challenge. He was surprised that for forty days no one had dared to go forth against the giant. He asked the men in the camp who this Philistine was to challenge God's army. David's older brother was angry, thinking David was causing trouble. David continued to ask the men why they would not battle Goliath when they had God on their side.

Saul heard about David and summoned him. David volunteered to fight Goliath. Saul denied David, saying he was too young. David told Saul that as a shepherd, he had single-handedly fought off both a lion and a bear when they had attacked his sheep. David said, "The Lord that delivered me out of the paw of lion, and out of the paw of the bear, he will deliver me out of the hand of this Philistine" (1 Samuel 17:37). Saul agreed to let David go, and suited him with armor, helmet, coat of mail and a sword. David rejected all of these things. He needed only his own sling and five small stones.

As David faced Goliath, the giant ridiculed him and the Israelites. David simply said, "Thou comest to me with a sword, and with a spear, and with a shield: but I come to thee in the name of the Lord of hosts, the God of the armies of Israel, whom thou hast defied. This day will the Lord deliver thee into mine hand; and I will smite thee" (1 Samuel 17:45–46). David ran out to meet Goliath, took a stone, and slung it at the giant. The stone struck Goliath in the forehead and he fell dead. David had calmly done what others feared to do. He knew without a doubt that the Lord was with him. That knowledge gave David the courage to do great things. We have that same knowledge and ability. When we trust in the Lord and do His will, we know that all things are possible.

Journal Prompt: David did not understand why the soldiers did not have the faith to know that God was on their side. What are some things you can do to simply and calmly go about Heavenly Father's work?

Activity: To remember the story of David and Goliath, make slingshot cookies. Using your favorite sugar cookie recipe (dough or ready-made), shape cookies into a Y shape. Bake as directed. As soon as the cookies come out of the oven, and while they are still hot, string a small piece of licorice between the tops of the Y to create the slingshot. Any kind of candy makes great stones, especially malt balls.

43. Responsibility

Definition: Legally or ethically accountable.

Song: "Dear to the Heart of the Shepherd" (*Hymns*, 221)

Scriptures: 1 Peter 5:2–4

Parable of the Lost Sheep
Luke 15:1–10

The Savior taught a valuable lesson in responsibility when He gave the parable of the lost sheep. He was teaching groups of people when He called to Him some publicans and sinners. These publicans were tax collectors for King Herod. They were so hated by the Jews that if a Jewish man became a publican, he would be excommunicated. When Jesus called these men to join Him, the Pharisees and scribes complained against Him.

Jesus turned to the Pharisees and scribes and told a parable. "What man of you, having an hundred sheep, if he lose one of them, doth not leave the ninety and nine in the wilderness, and go after that which is lost, until he find it?" (Luke 15:4). When one lost sheep is found, the shepherd rejoices over it. He calls together his friends and family and celebrates the return of the sheep that was missing.

Shepherds in Jesus' day stayed with their sheep vigilantly. They kept watch over them day and night to protect them against predators and other dangers. The shepherd knew each sheep individually and could tell if one was missing. If a sheep was lost, that shepherd would do all that was in his power to bring him back. He would not stop until he found the missing sheep and returned him safely to the fold. Then the shepherd's joy would be so great that he would celebrate.

Jesus was telling the scribes and Pharisees of His desire to find the "lost sheep" of the world, the sinners, and bring them back into the "fold" of our Heavenly Father's presence. He has given us this charge as well. If we are to be like Christ, we must be like a shepherd. We must diligently seek a lost sheep and do the Lord's work by sharing the gospel with them. These sheep may be thousands of miles away, or right next door as we serve our neighbors. We are all precious in our Father's eyes and, as the Savior said, "Likewise joy shall be in heaven over one sinner that repenteth" (Luke 15:10).

Journal Prompt: We have a responsibility to share the gospel. How can you be a missionary right now?

Activity: To demonstrate our responsibility to our neighbors, get pass-along cards and plan to hand them out whenever possible. Carry them with you in a wallet, purse, backpack, and so on. Be ready to share the gospel with opportunities to give the cards away.

44. Tolerance

Definition: The capacity for or practice of recognizing and respecting the opinions, practices, or behavior of others.

Song: "Nay, Speak No Ill" (*Hymns,* 233)

Scriptures: James 4:11; Ephesians 4:29–32; Hebrews 12:7

A Woman Anoints the Savior's Feet
Luke 7:36–50

*J*esus was traveling in the lands surrounding the Sea of Galilee. He had recently called Peter, the fisherman, to come and join Him in "catching men" instead of fish. Peter followed Jesus and became one of the twelve apostles. As they journeyed, Jesus taught, prophesied, healed, and raised a man from the dead. One of the Pharisees, Simon, who had been listening to Jesus, invited Him to eat at his home. Jesus went with him. As they ate their meal, a woman known in the city as a sinner came in. She came up behind Jesus with an alabaster box of oil for anointing, a sign of hospitality. The woman began to cry at Jesus' feet, spilling her tears on Him. She used her hair to wipe the tears from His feet. She kissed His feet and then anointed them with oil.

Simon saw the woman doing these things and thought to himself, "This man, if he were a prophet, would have known who and what manner of woman this is that toucheth him: for she is a sinner" (Luke 7:39).

Jesus turned him and said, "Simon, I have somewhat to say unto thee" (Luke 7:40). Simon asked Jesus to continue. The Savior related a story: Suppose there was a man who had loaned money to two people. Let's imagine one man owed five hundred dollars (the scriptures say five hundred pence, or denarii, which was a day's wages) and the other man owed fifty dollars. If neither man could pay his debt and the creditor (the man to whom they owed the money) freely forgave them both, which man would love the creditor most? Simon answered, "I suppose that he, to whom he forgave most" (v. 43). Jesus agreed with Simon.

Jesus then turned to the woman and said to Simon, "Seest thou this woman? I entered into thine house, thou gavest no water for my feet: but she hath washed my feet with her tears, and wiped them with the hairs of her head. Thou gavest me no kiss: but this woman since the time I came in hath not ceased to kiss my feet. My head with oil thou didst not anoint: but this woman hath anointed my feet with ointment. Wherefore I say unto thee, Her sins, which are many, are forgiven; for she loved much: but to whom little is forgiven, the same loveth little" (Luke 7:44–47).

There is a Primary song that says, "Jesus said love everyone; treat them kindly, too. When your heart is filled with love, others will love you" ("Jesus Said Love Everyone," *Children's Songbook,* 61). The Savior never said love everyone who is just like you. He told us to show kindness to all people. We are all children of our Heavenly Father, regardless of our circumstances. He showed us how to be tolerant to those who may not understand our beliefs or practices and to those who choose to live or act differently.

Journal Prompt: Are you tolerant of other people's beliefs? What can you do to be more tolerant of those around you? How will following the Savior help you accomplish this?

Activity: Have each member of the family wash and dry someone else's feet. This can be a very humbling, loving experience.

45. Friendliness

Definition: Favorably disposed; not antagonistic; warm; comforting.

Song: "Come Along, Come Along" (*Hymns*, 244)

Scriptures: Proverbs 27:9–10; Isaiah 53:3; Isaiah 61:1; D&C 121:9–10

Jonathan and David
1 Samuel 16–20

David was the Lord's choice to be king over His people. This position was, at that time, already held by Saul. Saul had turned away from the Lord and was no longer following Him, so the Lord had the prophet Samuel anoint David. David was just a shepherd boy when Samuel came to him, but he was filled with the Spirit of God.

Saul still sat on the throne, but he was plagued by an evil spirit. Saul's servants suggested perhaps some nice, soothing music would help. Saul commanded them to find someone to play for him. The servants searched for David, whom they knew to be a musician. David played a harp as he watched his family's sheep. He also wrote songs of praise to the Lord known as Psalms. The servants brought David before the king, and Saul was pleased. David came to play for the king whenever Saul was vexed. The music calmed Saul and "the evil spirit departed from him" (1 Samuel 16:23).

At this time, the Israelites were at war with the Philistines. David, the shepherd boy, defeated the nine-foot Philistine giant, Goliath, with only a slingshot and a stone. Saul was understandably impressed. He went to David's home and brought him back to live with him. David and Saul's son, Jonathan, became best friends. The scriptures say, "The soul of Jonathan was knit with the soul of David, and Jonathan loved him as his own soul" (1 Samuel 18:1). David did all that Saul required of him and "behaved himself wisely" (v. 5).

As Saul, David, and Jonathan returned to the city after a victory over the Philistines, women came out dancing and singing to greet them. The women cried out, "Saul hath slain his thousands, and David his ten thousands" (1 Samuel 18:7). These remarks made Saul jealous and angry and changed the relationship between Saul and David from that time forth.

Over the course of the next few years, David struggled with his feelings of loyalty to Saul and his fear of him. Saul made several attempts on David's life. On one occasion, David was only able to escape death when Jonathan pled with his father on David's behalf. David married Saul's daughter, Michal, who helped David escape yet another of Saul's plots. David had to run away. Before he left, he had a heart-wrenching conversation with Jonathan in which he asked, "What have I done? what is mine iniquity? and what is my sin before thy father that he seeketh my life?" (1 Samuel 20:1). Jonathan told David if his father was planning to kill David, he would know. David said Saul knew they were best friends and would, for that very reason, keep his plans from Jonathan. The two friends had an idea.

The next evening, David would be expected to dine with Saul, but he would hide out instead. He planned to do this for at least three nights, so Saul would be sure to notice his absence. Jonathan was to answer Saul's queries by telling him that David had asked permission to return home to Bethlehem for an annual sacrifice, and Jonathan had granted permission. If Saul responded favorably, it would indicate good feelings toward David on the part of the king. If, however, Saul was angry, Jonathan would know that the king still had evil designs.

The next thing to work out was how to alert David. They could not risk Jonathan being seen with David. They decided to have David hide behind a certain rock on the third day of his absence. Jonathan would bring his young servant with him to practice shooting arrows. He would shoot three arrows. If he had good news for David, Jonathan would shoot the arrows to the side of the rock and call out for his servant to retrieve them there. If Saul still sought to take David's life, Jonathan would shoot the arrows past the rock and shout for the boy to go out further to get them.

The next day, Jonathan came to the meal with his father. Saul noticed that David was not present, but he just assumed "something hath befallen him" (1 Samuel 20:26). On the second day, Saul again realized David was absent. He asked his son where David had been the last two days. Jonathan recited back the story that he and David had concocted. Saul was furious. He insulted Jonathan for allowing David to go and vowed to kill David. Jonathan asked what David's crimes were that he should be killed. Saul threw a javelin at Jonathan, attempting to murder him as well. Jonathan left in "fierce anger" (v. 34).

In the morning, Jonathan took his servant as planned and went to shoot. When they arrived at the spot, Jonathan told the boy to run and fetch the arrows after he shot them. Jonathan shot three arrows. The boy found the first two, and Jonathan called out after him, "Is not the arrow beyond thee? . . . Make speed, haste, stay not" (1 Samuel 20:26). The boy retrieved the arrow and came back to Jonathan none the wiser. Jonathan gave his servant the bow and arrows and told him to take them back. As soon as the boy had left, David arose from his hiding spot. David and Jonathan cried together, for they both knew that David had to leave. Jonathan said to David, "Go in peace, forasmuch as we have sworn both of us in the name of the Lord, saying, The Lord be between me and thee, and between my seed and thy seed for ever" (v. 42).

David and Jonathan's friendship was a bond so deep that they considered each other a brother. They would have defended one another to the death.

Note: You may want to read the touching words of David when he heard about Saul's and Jonathan's deaths in battle, found in 2 Samuel 1.

Journal Prompt: Friends are important. Write a list of qualities you think are valuable in a friend. Do you have these qualities? What can you do to be a better friend?

Activity: Make friendship bracelets for family members. Each bracelet will require at least two colors of embroidery floss. This floss is purchased for just a few cents in any craft store. Cut lengths of floss about eighteen inches. Each bracelet needs six of these lengths. Use any combination of color.

Tie all six strands together at one end, leaving the other ends free. Tape the tied end to a table or your knee. Separate the six strands. Beginning on the left, tie the first two strands together. Make sure to always keep the left strand over the right as you tie. Tie them together again. Using the same first strand, tie the first and third strands together. Tie them together again. Continue across the rest of the strands, always using that first strand, and working to the right.

When you have tied the first strand to the sixth strand twice, you will begin at the left again. Now the second strand will be in the first place. Keep moving across the bracelet to the right, tying knots twice on each strand. Once the bracelet is the length you want, tie the remaining strands together as you did at the beginning of the bracelet. Now tie the two ends together.

46. Honor

Definition: To respect or revere.

Song: "Praise to the Man" (*Hymns,* 27)

Scriptures: Exodus 20:12; D&C 135

Joseph Smith in Prison
D&C 121; *Autobiography,* by Parley Pratt

Note: In the interest of small children, there is only a brief overview of the Saints' persecution. Further discussion of events leading up to the prophet's imprisonment, such as Haun's Mill, is left to the discretion of individual families.

The early Saints continually had to leave their homes and families to travel to a land where they would have the freedom to follow the gospel of Jesus Christ as it had been restored through the Prophet Joseph Smith. As they were driven from one place to another, they suffered heartbreaking losses. Many people walked for hundreds of miles with no shoes and insufficient clothing to protect them from the elements. Men, women, and children died and were buried along the way.

The worst struggles, though, were the persecutions that were heaped upon the Saints by anti-Mormon mobs. People who only wanted to live peaceably were met with anger, prejudice, and hostility. When conditions made it too dangerous for the Saints to remain, they were forced to pack up their belongings and begin anew the search for a home.

These faithful pioneers followed the counsel of the Prophet as he inquired of the Lord on their behalf. Section 121 of the Doctrine and Covenants records the Prophet's pleas for the people. We can sense his agony as he prayed,

> O God, where art thou? And where is the pavilion that covereth thy hiding place?
>
> How long shall thy hand be stayed, and thine eye, yea thy pure eye, behold from the eternal heavens the wrongs of thy people and of thy servants, and thine ear be penetrated with their cries?
>
> Yea, O Lord, how long shall they suffer these wrongs and unlawful oppressions, before thine heart shall be softened toward them, and thy bowels be moved with compassion toward them?
>
> O Lord God Almighty, maker of heaven, earth, and seas, and of all things that in them are, and who controllest and subjectest the devil, and the dark and benighted dominion of Sheol—stretch forth thy hand; let thine eye pierce; let thy pavilion be taken up; let thy hiding place no longer be covered; let thine ear be inclined; let thine heart be softened, and thy bowels moved with compassion toward us.
>
> Let thine anger be kindled against our enemies; and, in the fury of thine heart, with thy sword avenge us of our wrongs.
>
> Remember thy suffering saints, O our God; and thy servants will rejoice in thy name forever. (vv. 1–6)

The Lord responded to the Prophet Joseph's appeal by saying, "My son, peace be unto thy soul; thine adversity and thine afflictions shall be but a small moment; And then, if thou endure it well, God shall exalt thee on high; thou shalt triumph over all thy foes" (vv. 7–8). These words of the Lord comforted and uplifted the Prophet so that he could endure his own afflictions as well. While unjustly imprisoned in Richmond Jail in Missouri, Joseph and other prisoners were subjected to cruel abuse at the hands of the guards. For two weeks this went on. One evening the guards were taunting the prisoners with "obscene jests, the horrid oaths, the dreadful blasphemies and filthy language" for hours (*Autobiography*, 169). The guards began to describe the atrocities which had been committed against the Saints. Parley Pratt says he lay there listening to these jeers until he felt he could no longer stand it, when Joseph Smith stood up in shackles and reprimanded the guards. In a "voice of thunder" Joseph said: "SILENCE, ye fiends of the infernal pit. In the name of Jesus Christ I rebuke you, and command you to be still; I will not live another minute and bear such language. Cease such talk, or you or I die THIS INSTANT!" (169–170).

Parley Pratt says of the Prophet, "He ceased to speak. He stood erect in terrible majesty. Chained and without a weapon; calm, unruffled and dignified as an angel, he looked upon the qualing guards, whose weapons were lowered or dropped to the ground; whose knees smote together, and who, shrinking into a corner, or crouching at his feet, begged his pardon, and remained quiet till a change of guards" (*Autobiography*, 179).

The Prophet was filled with the Spirit of the Lord. He did not need to scream and shout to be heard. He accomplished more with a quiet sense of honor than he could have in any other way. Parley Pratt said it best: "Dignity and majesty have I seen but *once*, as it stood in chains, at midnight, in a dungeon in an obscure village of Missouri" (*Autobiography*, 179).

Journal Prompt: What does "a sense of honor" mean to you? What is something you would be willing to stand up for?

Activity: Draw or paint a picture of the jail scene to add to your Virtue Scrapbook.

47. Love

Definition: A strong affection for another person; the feeling of benevolence, kindness, or brotherhood toward others.

Song: "O Love That Glorifies the Son" (*Hymns,* 295)

Scriptures: Moroni 7:45–48; John 17:20–23

The Atonement
Mark 15

This is part of the story of the Atonement. Just as that of the Garden of Gethsemane, the trial, mocking, and Crucifixion are more powerful than words could adequately convey. Please take this opportunity in your family home evening to read Mark's account of our Savior's suffering, sacrifice, and hence His great love for us directly from the scriptures. Sometimes it seems as if younger children do not comprehend the more difficult language of the scriptures; however, in this story especially, the Spirit can be felt so strongly and can testify to us all, regardless of age.

Journal Prompt: It is hard to understand how completely our Savior loves us. How can we show our love for Him and our gratitude for His atoning sacrifice?

Activity: Make a "Love Poster" to hang in your home. Draw a giant heart in red on a plain sheet of poster board and hang the poster in a visible spot. Throughout the week, have family members write little notes of love to one another and post them on the board. It is wonderful to see faces light up when they read of their brother or sister's love for them!

48. Loyalty

Definition: Feelings of devoted attachment and affection

Song: "Stand for the Right" (*Children's Songbook,* 159)

Scriptures: Alma 53:20–21; Mormon 9:28; D&C 20:19; D&C 106:3

"For Wither Thou Goest, I Will Go"
Ruth 1–2

There was a great famine in the land of Israel. Many people had to leave their homes in search of food. One such family was led by a man named Elimelech. Elimelech's wife was Naomi, and they had two sons, Mahlon and Chilion. This family left Bethlehem and traveled to the land of Moab (see Bible Map 1: Physical Map of the Holy Land). The people of Moab were related to Israelites, and they spoke a similar language, but there was continual tension between the two peoples.

Once the family arrived in Moab, Elimelech died. Mahlon and Chilion married Moabite women, Orpah and Ruth. Shortly thereafter, Mahlon and Chilion also died. Naomi decided to return to her home in the land of Judah. Her daughters-in-law began the journey with her, but Naomi said to them, "Go, return each to her mother's house: the Lord deal kindly with you, as ye have dealt with the dead, and with me. The Lord grant you that ye may find rest, each of you in the house of her husband" (Ruth 1:8–9). Naomi kissed them and Orpah and Ruth cried. The women told Naomi that they would return to Judah with her. Naomi responded saying, "Turn again, my daughters: why will ye go with me?

Are there yet any more sons in my womb, that they may be your husbands?" (v. 11). In ancient times, the law stated that if a woman's husband died, she could only remarry within her husband's family. Naomi knew that she must send the girls back to their parents to live. Orpah and Ruth cried again. Orpah kissed Naomi and departed, but Ruth stood firm. Naomi told Ruth to go and follow after her sister-in-law, but Ruth said, "Intreat me not to leave thee, or to return from following after thee: for whither thou goest, I will go; and where thou lodgest, I will lodge: thy people shall be my people, and thy God my God: Where thou diest, will I die, and there will I be buried: the Lord do so to me, and more also, if ought but death part thee and me" (vv. 16–17).

And so Ruth and Naomi traveled together to Bethlehem. There lived a wealthy man named Boaz who was related to Naomi's husband, Elimelech. Boaz owned many fields of grain that his servants were harvesting. People were allowed to glean, or pick up the remnants of, the grain after the reapers cut and gathered it. Ruth asked Naomi if she could go into the fields after the reapers and glean. Naomi consented. It just so happened that Ruth ended up in the fields of Boaz. He came out to his fields and saw Ruth. He asked his servants about her, and they told him she was Naomi's widowed daughter-in-law from Moab. Boaz came to Ruth and told her to continue in his fields as she wished. Furthermore, he instructed her to drink from his water vessels whenever she was thirsty and to stay with his maidservants. Ruth fell to the ground in gratitude, asking Boaz what she had done to warrant his kindness. Boaz replied, "The Lord recompense thy work, and a full reward be given thee of the Lord God of Israel, under whose wings thou art come to trust" (Ruth 2:11–12).

Boaz and Ruth eventually married, with Naomi's blessing. They had a son named Obed, who had a son named Jesse, who had a son named David, who became one of the greatest kings in Israel's history. Ruth's loyalty was a blessing to Naomi, Boaz, and countless generations.

Journal Prompt: Family loyalty is an important thing. What are some of the things you like best about your family? What can you do to strengthen your family bond?

Activity: Hold an annual family birthday party to celebrate your ancestors. Tell any stories you may know about them, display pictures, and serve traditional family dishes for dinner. Don't forget to have birthday cake!

49. Sympathy

Definition: The act of or capacity for sharing or understanding the feelings of another person.

Song: "Truth Reflects upon Our Senses" (*Hymns,* 273)

Scriptures: Matthew 5:44; Alma 41:14–15

The Mote versus the Beam
JST—Matthew 7:1–5

Jesus chose a few specific topics to use in closing His Sermon on the Mount. One of these topics was the admonition to avoid judging others.

The Savior said, "And why beholdest thou the mote that is in thy brother's eye, but considerest not the beam that is in thine own eye?" (Matthew 7:3). A mote is a "speck, chip, or splinter" and a beam "refers to a wooden beam used in constructing houses" (v. 3, footnotes b and c). These two pieces of wood certainly are quite different in size. The Lord tells us we should not be so quick to notice the flaws in other people when we are quite flawed ourselves. For example, imagine a young boy, John, and his sister, Amy, are playing in the backyard. John teases Amy all afternoon. He makes fun of how she runs and picks on her about the way she laughs. Later that evening, the children are playing with their younger brother, Michael. When Amy teases Michael about his lisp, John tells their mother that Amy is being mean and should be punished. While Amy was wrong to pick on her little brother, did John behave any better earlier in the day? John was guilty of seeing the mote in Amy's eye without noticing the beam in his own.

Jesus went on to say, "Thou hypocrite, first cast out the beam out of thine own eye; and then shalt thou see clearly to cast out the mote out of thy brother's eye" (Matthew 7:5). How can we possibly help anyone with their imperfections until we have dealt with our own? We are all striving for perfection because our Savior told us, "Be ye therefore perfect, even as your Father which is in heaven is perfect" (Matthew 5:48). No one on this earth has reached that goal yet, though. For us to judge others would be very hypocritical.

One important aspect of our church is "perfecting the Saints." This is done through love and support of one another. We can pray for each other, encourage each other, and serve each other.

Jesus told His apostles, "Judge not unrighteously, that ye be not judged: but judge righteous judgment" (JST—Matthew 7:1). There are those who are called by God to positions that require making righteous judgments. For the rest of us; though, judging others has no place in our pursuit of living a Christlike life.

Instead of judging others, we can be sympathetic. We can notice and respond to the needs of others with genuine concern. When John heard Amy teasing their little brother about his lisp, John should have recognized his own faults and recognized he had set a bad example by being unkind earlier that day. John could have then encouraged Amy to be considerate of their younger brother's feelings. If this had happened, John would have improved himself and strengthened his bonds with Amy and Michael as well. When we work on our own imperfections and lovingly assist others, we are letting the light of Christ shine within us.

Journal Prompt: Have you ever heard the expression, "People in glass houses should not throw stones"? What do you think this means?

Activity: Small children in sacrament meeting often make a lot of noise. The mothers of those little children sometimes feel embarrassed by this. To show sympathy, make a present to help—a simple and inexpensive "quiet book." Stack five plastic zipper storage bags together with the zipper end on the right side. Stitch the bags together with needle and thread on the left side, with ⅜-inch seam allowance. Cut out or print from the Church website pictures from the *Friend* to put inside the zippered bags. Give these books to parents of young children in your ward.

50. Submission

Definition: In a state of yielding or surrendering oneself to the will or authority of another.

Song: "Be Thou Humble" (*Hymns,* 130)

Scriptures: D&C 112:10; Ether 12:27

Jonah
Jonah 1–4

There is a pattern in the scriptures of how the Lord deals with His people. When they follow the commandments, He blesses them. When they fall into unrighteousness, He does not immediately punish them. He sends a prophet to remind the people of their blessings and to encourage them to repent of their wrongdoings. If the people choose to remain in sin, then are they punished.

Roughly eight hundred years before the birth of Christ, there was a city immersed in wickedness called Ninevah (see Bible Map 9: The Assyrian Empire). Ninevah was the capital of Assyria and an enormous city. The Lord called the prophet Jonah to go to this city to preach repentance to the people. Instead of following this direction, Jonah ran away. He went to Joppa (see Bible Map 10: The World of the Old Testament) and bought passage on a boat to Tarshish in Spain. Jonah thought he could escape the Lord's will by going far away.

Once the boat had left port, a terrible storm arose. The winds were so terrible that the men on board cried out to their gods. They asked Jonah to pray to his God as well. The men then cast lots so they could figure out who was to blame for this storm. The lot fell on Jonah. Jonah told the sailors that God was displeased with him for shirking his responsibility. He told them that it was his fault the storm was raging, and they should throw him overboard to save their lives. The men tried their best to row to shore, but they could not make it. Their boat was nearly torn apart. Finally, they agreed to put Jonah into the sea. The men cried out, "O Lord, we beseech thee, let us not perish for this man's life, and lay not upon us innocent blood: for thou, O Lord, hast done as it pleased thee" (Jonah 1:14). As soon as Jonah had been set in the water, the storm stopped.

Jonah was swallowed up by a great fish. He remained in the belly of the fish for three days and three nights. Jonah prayed to the Lord for forgiveness and vowed to follow Him in the future. The Lord caused the fish to spit Jonah up on the shore.

Jonah was once again commanded to go to Ninevah to cry repentance to the people. This time he obeyed. Jonah entered the city of wickedness and told the people that they must stop sinning and obey God. "So the people of Nineveh believed God, and proclaimed a fast. . . . And God saw their works, that they turned from their evil way; and God turned away the evil that he had said he bring upon them" (Jonah 3:5, 10; see footnote 10c).

Jonah ran from the task he was given because he knew that the people of Ninevah were sinful. He did not feel they were worthy of being saved. What Jonah failed to realize is that all men, women, and children are precious in the sight of God. We are all children of our Heavenly Father.

Sometimes we are given jobs to do that we may not understand. When a call comes from the Lord, however, we should respond with faith. We do not see things as Heavenly Father does. When we submit ourselves to the will of the Lord, we can become an instrument in His hands.

Journal Prompt: Have you ever felt prompted to do something the Lord wanted you to do? What would you do if you received a calling or assignment that you were afraid of?

Activity: Study the latest general conference addresses as a family. Choose at least one thing from the counsel of the speakers to work on improving in your lives.

51. Fairness

Definition: Just to all parties; equitable; consistent with rules, logic, or ethics.

Song: "Help Me Teach with Inspiration" (*Hymns,* 281)

Scriptures: Alma 29:8; Articles of Faith 1:13

King Benjamin
Mosiah 1–5

King Benjamin was known to be a righteous man, a strong leader, and a fair ruler. At the end of his reign, King Benjamin appointed his son Mosiah to be the new king. Benjamin asked Mosiah to gather their people together at the temple so the king could address them a final time. The people came and they pitched tents by the temple doors in order to hear their king. The crowd was so large that King Benjamin ordered the building of a tower. The multitude was so great that, even up on the tower, King Benjamin's words could not be heard by many of the people. The king had his message written out and distributed among those who could not hear him.

King Benjamin addressed many topics that were of concern to his people, and many remain pertinent today. We are fortunate to have his counsel recorded in the Book of Mormon. He began by telling his people that he had tried to be a good and fair king. Instead of living off of their taxes and burdening them with heavy tasks, he had worked alongside them. He had tried to serve them well. King Benjamin was quick to say that he was not boasting in these remarks, but was trying to explain that he was serving God as he served the people. He said, "And behold, I tell you these things that ye may learn wisdom; that ye may learn that when ye are in the service of your fellow beings ye are only in the service of your God" (Mosiah 2:17). He went on to tell the people that if he deserved their thanks and praise for his service to them, then how much more should they thank and praise God for all He had given them. King Benjamin reminded the people that all the Lord required in return for His goodness was that they obey His commandments.

King Benjamin trembled as he announced that he could no longer be their king. His age made it difficult even to stand and speak to the people, but the Lord blessed him to continue. He warned them against allowing contention to arise among the people. He told them to remember Heavenly Father and to repent of any sins.

King Benjamin continued to instruct his people by telling them to care for one another. He said if they lived Christlike lives, they would live in peace. He encouraged his people to support those less fortunate than themselves.

In closing, King Benjamin asked the people if they believed what he had told them. "And they all cried with one voice, saying: Yea, we believe all the words which thou hast spoken unto us; and also, we know of their surety and truth, because of the Spirit of the Lord Omnipotent, which has wrought a mighty change in us, or in our hearts, that we have no more disposition to do evil, but to do good continually" (Mosiah 5:2).

King Benjamin affected the lives of countless men, women, and children for good because of the kind of ruler and man he was. He led his people in righteousness and left a legacy of fairness.

Journal Prompt: King Benjamin led his people in fairness. Today we have many Church leaders who lead and guide us. What are some of the things you like about your branch president or bishop? Do you think it is easy to lead a branch or ward?

Activity: Act out King Benjamin's sermon, taking turns being King Benjamin. Let each person teach a principle that King Benjamin taught.

52. Vigilance

Definition: Alert watchfulness.

Song: "I'll Go Where You Want Me to Go" (*Hymns*, 270)

Scriptures: Isaiah 52:7–8; Matthew 25:13; D&C 4:2

Noah and the Ark
Genesis 6–9; Moses 8

Adam and Eve's great-great-great-great-great-great-great-grandson was Noah. That is seven generations. Noah was an obedient follower of God. He was ordained to the priesthood at the age of ten and became a prophet later in his life.

As an adult of nearly six hundred years, Noah went about preaching repentance to the wicked people of his time. "And God saw that the wickedness of man was great in the earth, and that every imagination of the thoughts of his heart was only evil continually" (Genesis 6:5). The Lord was very sad with the way His children had chosen to live. He did not want this wickedness to continue, so He said, "I will destroy man whom I have created from the face of the earth; both man and beast, and the creeping thing, and the fowls of the air; for it repenteth me that I have made them" (v. 7). The word *repenteth* is used here to mean "to be sorry." There was such evil in the world that the Lord was sorry He had created man.

Our Father in Heaven always gives us an opportunity to turn from sin and repent. And so Noah received instruction from the Lord to proclaim the gospel to the people. But the people chose not to listen to Noah. Their hearts were hardened against God and they wanted to continue living their own way. The Lord said, "The end of all flesh is come before me; for the earth is filled with violence, and behold I will destroy them with the earth" (Genesis 6:13).

The Lord told Noah to make an ark, or boat, of gopher wood. This was probably the wood of the cypress tree, which produced a kind of resin, or glue-like substance. Noah was given specific building instructions, including the dimensions of the ark. It was to be three hundred cubits, (four hundred fifty feet) long; fifty cubits, (seventy-three feet) wide; and thirty cubits, or about three stories high. There was to be a window and a door. The ark was divided into rooms on three floors. Noah did as the Lord had commanded. He knew there was great destruction coming to the earth.

The floods came. "The windows of heaven were opened. And the rain was upon the earth forty days and forty nights" (Genesis 7:11–12). All the earth was covered with water and every living creature outside the ark died. The waters covered the earth for 150 days. The ark came to rest on the mountains called Ararat (see Bible Map 9: The World of the Old Testament). Many people are still searching for the exact location of the ark today.

After three months, the tops of the mountains were once again visible. Forty days later, Noah sent out a dove to see if there was any dry land. The dove found no place to land, and returned to the ark. Seven days later, Noah tried sending out the dove again. "And the dove came in to him in the evening; and, lo, in her mouth was an olive leaf pluckt off: so Noah knew that the waters were abated from off the earth" (Genesis 8:11). Noah sent the dove out one more time seven days later. This time the dove did not return.

The Lord told Noah that it was now safe to leave the ark. He told Noah to take the animals from the ark and set them free to repopulate the earth. Noah did as he was told and then built an altar to the Lord.

Long ago, the Lord cleansed the earth of evil and corruption with a flood that covered the entire planet. He has promised that a flood of that magnitude would never happen again. We are reminded of this promise every time we see the beauty of a rainbow.

Being vigilant is being alert and watchful. We must be alert to what the prophet commands us to do. Noah preached to the people, trying to convince them to soften their hearts and follow the Lord. He did all that he was commanded to do. Noah and his family were blessed for their vigilance.

Journal Prompt: Noah was the watchman in his day. Today we have a prophet as well. Do you think we listen as we should to our watchman? How can you better follow the prophet?

Activity: Discuss the need for and the prophet's counsel on food storage. Assess your family's food and water storage situation. Talk about food rotation. Make a plan to add to your storage as needed.

APPENDIX: Silhouette pattern for Commitment activity, page 7.

References

Children's Songbook. Salt Lake City: The Church of Jesus Christ of Latter-day Saints, 1989.

Hymns of The Church of Jesus Christ of Latter-day Saints. Salt Lake City: The Church of Jesus Christ of Latter-day Saints, 1985.

Pratt, Parley P. *Autobiography.* Salt Lake City: Deseret Book, 1985.

"101 Sabbath Day Activities." LightPlanet.com. Used with permission for filmstrip activity for chapter 6.

About the Author

*L*ily Stainback grew up and still lives in eastern North Carolina. She met her husband, Jay, on a blind date set up by his dad. They have four children: Nick, 15; Rachael, 12; Wil, 11; and Faith, 8. They have been home schooling their children for nine years. The Stainbacks enjoy playing games, cooking together, karaoke, animals, and anything at the beach.